Thomas Gray

The Poetical Works of Thomas Gray

With the Life of the Author

Thomas Gray

The Poetical Works of Thomas Gray
With the Life of the Author

ISBN/EAN: 9783744794534

Printed in Europe, USA, Canada, Australia, Japan

Cover: Foto ©Thomas Meinert / pixelio.de

More available books at **www.hansebooks.com**

GRAY'S POEMS.

Approach & read, for thou canst read, the lay
Grav'd on the stone beneath yon aged thorn.

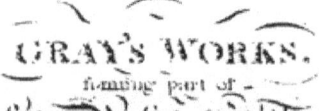

GRAY'S WORKS,

forming part of

Cooke's Pocket Edition of

the Original & Complete Works of

SELECT BRITISH POETS,

or Entertaining Poetical Library,

containing the most Esteemed

Poetic Productions,

Superbly Embellished.

THE POETICAL WORKS OF THOMAS GRAY.

WITH THE LIFE OF THE AUTHOR.

Cooke's Edition.

> Thy form benign, oh, Goddess! wear,
> Thy milder influence impart,
> To soften, not to wound, my heart:
> The gen'rous spark extinct revive,
> Teach me to love and to forgive;
> Exact my own defects to scan,
> What others are to feel, and know my-
>   self a man.]   *Ode to Adversity.*

> Too poor for a bribe, and too proud to importune,
> He had not the method of making a fortune;
> Could love and could hate, so was thought somewhat odd;
> No very great wit; he believ'd in a God;
> A post or a pension he did not desire,
> But left church and state to Charles Townshend and Squire.
>   *Gray of Himself.*

EMBELLISHED WITH SUPERB ENGRAVINGS.

London:

Printed for C. COOKE, No. 17, Paternoster-Row;
And sold by all the Booksellers in
Great Britain and
Ireland.

THE POETICAL WORKS OF THOMAS GRAY.

CONTAINING HIS

ODES, MISCELLANIES,

&c. &c. &c.

Hark! the Fatal Sisters join----
Hail, ye Midnight Sisters! hail----
O'er the glory of the land,
O'r the innocent and gay,
O'er the Muses' tuneful band,
Weave the fun'ral web of *Gray.*
'Tis done-----'tis done-----
He sinks, he groans, he falls, a lifeless corse----
O'er his green grave, in Contemplation's guise,
Oft' let the pilgrim drop a silent tear,
Oft' let the shepherd's tender accents rise,
Big with the sweets of each revolving year,
Till prostrate Time adore his deathless name,
Fix'd on the solid base of adamantine fame.

J. T. to Mem. of Gray.

London:
PRINTED AND EMBELLISHED
Under the Direction of
C. COOKE.

COOKE'S EDITION OF SELECT POETS.

GRAY.

THE LIFE OF
THOMAS GRAY.

THOMAS GRAY was born in Cornhill, in the city of London, on the 26th of December, 1716. His father, Philip Gray, was a money-scrivener; but being of an indolent and profuse disposition, he rather diminished than improved his paternal fortune. Our Author received his classical education at Eton school, under Mr. Antrobus, his mother's brother, a man of sound learning and refined taste, who directed his nephew to those pursuits which laid the foundation of his future literary fame.

During his continuance at Eton, he contracted a friendship with Mr. Horace Walpole, well known for his knowledge in the fine arts; and Mr. Richard West, son of the Lord Chancellor of Ireland, a youth of very promising talents.

When he left Eton school in 1734, he went to Cambridge, and entered a pensioner at Peterhouse, at the recommendation of his uncle Antrobus, who had been a fellow of that college. It is said that, from his effeminacy and fair complexion, he acquired, among his fellow students, the appellation of *Miss* Gray, to which the delicacy of his manners seems not a little to have contributed. Mr. Walpole was at that time a fellow-commoner of King's College, in the same University; a fortunate circumstance, which afforded Gray frequent opportunities of intercourse with his Honourable Friend.

Mr. West went from Eton to Christ Church, Oxford; and in this state of separation, these two votaries of the Muses, whose dispositions were congenial, commenced an epistolary correspondence, part of which is published by Mr. Mason, a gentleman whose character stands high in the republic of letters.

Gray, having imbibed a taste for poetry, did not relish those abstruse studies which generally occupy the minds of students at College; and therefore, as he found very little gratification from academical pursuits, he left Cambridge in 1738, and returned to London, intending to apply himself to the study of the law: but this intention was soon laid aside, upon an invitation given him by Mr. Walpole, to accompany him in his travels abroad; a situation highly preferable, in Gray's opinion, to the dry study of the law.

They set out together for France, and visited most of the places worthy of notice in that country: from thence they proceeded to Italy, where an unfortunate dispute taking place between them, a separation ensued upon their arrival at Florence. Mr. Walpole afterwards, with great candour and liberality, took upon himself the blame of the quarrel; though, if we consider the matter coolly and impartially, we may be induced to conclude that Gray, from a conscious superiority of ability, might have claimed a deference to his opinion and judgment, which his Honourable Friend was not at that time disposed to admit: the rupture, however, was very unpleasant to both parties.

Gray pursued his journey to Venice on an economic plan, suitable to the circumscribed state of his finances; and having continued there some weeks, returned to England in September, 1741. He appears, from his letters, published by Mr. Mason, to have paid the minutest attention to every object worthy of notice throughout the course of his travels. His descriptions are lively and picturesque, and bear particular marks of his genius and disposition. We admire the sublimity of his ideas when he ascends the stupendous heights of the Alps, and are charmed with his display of nature, decked in all the beauties of vegetation. Indeed, abundant information, as well as entertainment, may be derived from his casual letters.

In about two months after his arrival in England, he lost his father, who, by an indiscreet profusion, had so impaired his fortune, as not to admit of his son's prosecuting the study of the law with that degree of respectability which the nature of the profession requires, without becoming burthensome to his mother and aunt. To obviate, therefore, their importunities on the subject, he went to Cambridge, and took his bachelor's degree in civil law.

But the inconveniencies and distress attached to a scanty fortune were not the only ills our Poet had to encounter at this time: he had not only lost the friendship of Mr. Walpole abroad, but poor West, the partner of his heart, fell a victim to complicated maladies, brought on by family misfortunes, on the 1st of June, 1742, at Popes, a village, in Hertfordshire, where he went for the benefit of the air.

The excessive degree in which his mind was agitated for the loss of his friend, will best appear from the following beautiful little sonnet:

"In vain to me the smiling mornings shine,
"And redd'ning Pœbus lifts his golden fire:
"The birds in vain their am'rous descant join,
"Or cheerful fields resume their green attire:
"These ears, alas! for other notes repine;
"A different object do these eyes require;
"My lonely anguish melts no heart but mine,
"And in my breast th' imperfect joys expire;
"Yet morning smiles the busy race to cheer,
"And new-born pleasure brings to happier men;
"The fields to all their wonted tribute bear;
"To warn their little loves the birds complain:
"I fruitless mourn to him that cannot hear;
"And weep the more, because I weep in vain."

Mr. Gray now seems to have applied his mind very sedulously to poetical composition: his *Ode to Spring* was written early in June, to his friend Mr. West, before he received the melancholy news of his death: how our Poet's susceptible mind was affected by that melancholy incident, is evidently demonstrated by the lines quoted above; the impression, indeed, appears to have been too deep to be soon effaced; and the tenour of the subjects which called for the exertions of his poetical talents subsequent to the production of this Ode, corroborates that observation; these were his *Prospect of Eton*, and his *Ode to Adversity*. It is also supposed, and with great probability, that he began his *Elegy in a Country Church Yard* about the same time. He passed some weeks at Stoke, near Windsor, where his mother and aunt resided, and in that pleasing retirement finished several of his most celebrated Poems.

From thence he returned to Cambridge, which, from this period, was his chief residence during the remainder of his life. The conveniencies with which a college life was attended, to a person of his narrow fortune, and studious turn of mind, were more than a compensation for the dislike which, for several reasons, he bore to the place: but he was perfectly reconciled to his situation, on Mr. Mason's being elected a fellow of Pembroke-Hall; a circumstance which brought him a companion, who, during life, retained for him the highest degree of friendship and esteem.

In 1742 he was admittted to the degree of Batchelor in the Civil Law, as appears from a letter written to his particular friend Dr. Wharton, of Old Park, near Durham, formerly fellow of Pembroke Hall, Cambridge, in which he ridicules, with much point and humour, the follies and foibles, and the dullness and formality, which prevailed in the University.

In order to enrich his mind with the ideas of others, he devoted a considerable portion of his time to the study of the best Geeek authors; so that, in the course of six years, there were hardly any writers of eminence in that language whose works he had not only read, but thoroughly digested.

His attention, however, to the Greek classics, did not wholly engross his time; for he found leisure to advert, in a new farcaftical manner, to the ignorance and dullnefs with which he was furrounded, though fituated in the centre of learning. There is only a fragment remaining of what he had written on this fubject, from which it may be inferred, that it was intended as an *Hymn to Ignorance.* The fragment is wholly introductory; yet many of the lines are fo pointed in fignification, and harmonious in verfification, that they will be admitted, by the admirers of verfe, to difplay his poetical talents with more brilliancy than appears in many of his lyric productions.

Hail, horrors, hail! ye ever gloomy bowers,
Ye Gothic fanes, and antiquated towers!
Where rufhy Camus' flowly-winding flood
Perpetual draws his humid train of mud:
Glad I revifit thy neglected reign:
Oh, take me to thy peaceful fhade again:
But chiefly thee, whofe influence, breath'd from high,
Augments the native darknefs of the fky.
Ah, Ignorance! foft, falutary power!
Proftrate with filial reverence I adore.
Thrice hath Hyperion roll'd his annual race,
Since weeping I forfook thy fond embrace.
Oh, fay, fuccefsful doft thou ftill oppofe,
Thy leaden Ægis 'gainft our ancient foes?
Still ftretch, tenacious of thy right divine,
The maffy fceptre o'er thy flumbering line?
And dews Lethean through the land difpenfe,
To fteep in flumbers each benighted fenfe?
If any fpark of wit's delufive ray
Break out, and flafh a momentary day,
With damp, cold touch forbid it to afpire,
And huddle up in fogs the dangerous fire.
Oh, fay----She hears me not, but, carelefs grown,
Lethargic nods upon her ebon throne.
Goddefs! awake, arife; alas! my fears;
Can powers immortal feel the force of years?
Not thus of old, with enfigns wide unfurl'd,
She rode triumphant o'er the vanquifh'd world:
Fierce nations own'd her unrefifted might;
And all was ignorance, and all was night!
Oh facred age! Oh times for ever loft!
(The fchoolman's glory, and the churchman's boaft,)
For ever gone---yet ftill to fancy new,
Her rapid wings the tranfient fcene purfue,
And bring the buried ages back to view.
  High on her car, behold the grandam ride,
Like old Sefoftris with barbaric pride;
***** a team of harnefs'd monarchs' bend
*****

In

In 1744 he seems to have given up his attention to the Muses. Mr. Walpole, desirous of preserving what he had already written, as well as perpetuating the merit of their deceased friend, West, endeavoured to prevail with Gray, to whom he had previously become reconciled, to publish his own Poems, together with those of West; but Gray declined it, conceiving their productions united would not suffice to fill even a small volume.

In 1747 Gray became acquainted with Mr. Mason, then a scholar of St. John's College, and afterwards Fellow of Pembroke Hall. Mr. Mason, who was a man of great learning and ingenuity, had written, the year before, his "Monody on the Death of Pope," and his "Il Bellicoso, and "Il Pacifico;" and Gray revised these pieces at the request of a friend. This laid the foundation of a friendship that terminated but with life: and Mr. Mason, after the death of Gray, testified his regard for him, by superintending the publication of his works.

The same year he wrote a little Ode on the Death of a favourite Cat of Mr. Walpole's, in which humour and instruction are happily blended: but the following year he produced an effort of much more importance; the Fragment of an *Essay on the Alliance of Education and Government*. Its tendency was to demonstrate the necessary concurrence of both to form great and useful Men. It opens with the two following similies. The exordium is rather uncommon; but he seems to have adopted it as a kind of clue to the subject he meant to pursue in the subsequent part of the Poem.

As sickly plants betray a niggard earth,
Whose barren bosom starves her gen'rous birth,
Nor genial warmth nor genial juice retains,
Their roots to feed and fill their verdant veins;
And as in climes, where Winter holds his reign,
The soil, tho' fertile, will not teem in vain,
Forbids her gems to swell, her shades to rise,
Nor trusts her blossoms to the churlish skies;
So draw mankind in vain the vital airs,
Unform'd, unfriended, by those kindly cares

That health and vigour to the foul impart,
Spread the young thought, and warm the op'ning heart;
So fond inftruction on the growing pow'rs
Of Nature idly lavifhes her ftores,
If equal Juftice, with unclouded face,
Smile not indulgent on the rifing race,
And fcatter with a free, tho' frugal hand,
Light golden fhow'rs of plenty o'er the land:
But Tyranny has fix'd her empire there,
To check their tender hopes with chilling fear,
And blaft the blooming promife of the year.

This fpacious animated fcene furvey,
From where the rolling orb, that gives the day,
His fable fons with nearer courfe furrounds
To either pole and life's remoteft bounds;
How rude foe'er th' exterior form we find,
Howe'er opinion tinge the vary'd mind,
Alike to all the kind impartial Heav'n
The fparks of truth and happinefs has given;
With fenfe to feel, with mem'ry to retain,
They follow pleafure and they fly from pain;
Their judgment mends the plan their fancy draws,
Th' event prefages and explores the caufe;
The foft returns of gratitude they know,
By fraud elude, by force repel, the foe;
While mutual wifhes mutual woes endear,
The focial fmile and fympathetic tear.

Say, then, thro' ages by what fate confin'd
To diff'rent climes feem diff'rent fouls affign'd;
Here meafur'd laws and philofophic eafe
Fix and improve the polifh'd arts of peace;
There Induftry and Gain their vigils keep,
Command the winds and tame th' unwilling deep:
Here force and hardy deeds of blood prevail,
There languid Pleafure fighs in ev'ry gale.
Oft' o'er the trembling nations from afar
Has Scythia breath'd the living cloud of war;
And where the deluge burft with fweepy fway,
Their arms, their kings, their gods, were roll'd away:
As oft' have iffu'd, hoft impelling hoft,
The blue-ey'd myriads from the Baltic coaft;
The proftrate South to the deftroyer yields
Her boafted titles and her golden fields:
With grim delight the brood of Winter view
A brighter day, and heav'ns of azure hue,
Scent the new fragrance of the breathing rofe,
And quaff the pendent vintage as it grows.
Proud of the yoke, and pliant to the rod,
Why yet does Afia dread a monarch's nod,
While European freedom ftill withftands
Th' encroaching tide that drowns her lefs'ning lands,
And fees far off, with an indignant groan,
Her native plains and empires once her own?
Can op'ner fkies, and fons of fiercer flame,
O'erpower the fire that animates our frame;
As lamps, that fhed at eve a cheerful ray,
Fade and expire beneath the eye of day?

> Need we the influence of the northern ſtar
> To ſtring our nerves and ſteel our hearts to war?
> And where the face of Nature laughs around,
> Muſt ſick'ning Virtue fly the tainted ground?
> Unmanly thought! what ſeaſons can controul.
> What fancy'd zone can circumſcribe, the ſoul,
> Who, conſcious of the ſource from whence ſhe ſprings,
> By Reaſon's light, on Reſolution's wings,
> Spite of her frail companion, dauntleſs goes
> O'er Lybia's deſerts and thro' Zembla's ſnows?
> She bids each ſlumb'ring energy awake,
> Another touch another temper take,
> Suſpends th' inferior laws that rule our clay;
> The ſtubborn elements confeſs her ſway;
> Their little wants their low deſires refine,
> And raiſe the mortal to a height divine.
>
> Not but the human fabric from the birth
> Imbibes a flavour of its parent earth;
> As various tracts enforce a various toil,
> The manners ſpeak the idiom of their ſoil.
> An iron race the mountain-cliffs maintain,
> Foes to the gentler genius of the plain;
> For where unweary'd ſinews muſt be found
> With ſide-long plough to quell the flinty ground,
> To turn the torrent's ſwift-deſcending flood,
> To brave the ſavage ruſhing from the wood,
> What wonder if, to patient valour train'd,
> They guard with ſpirit what by ſtrength they gain'd?
> And while their rocky ramparts round they ſee,
> The rough abode of Want and Liberty,
> (As lawleſs force from confidence will grow)
> Inſult the plenty of the vales below?
> What wonder in the ſultry climes, that ſpread
> Where Nile, redundant o'er his ſummer-bed,
> From his broad boſom life and verdure flings,
> And broods o'er Ægypt. with his wat'ry wings,
> If, with advent'rous oar and ready ſail,
> The duſky people drive before the gale,
> Or on frail floats to neighbouring cities ride,
> That riſe and glitter o'er the ambient tide?
> * * * * * * *

It is much to be lamented that our Author did not finiſh what was ſo ſucceſsfully begun, as the Fragment is deemed ſuperior to every thing in the ſame ſtyle of writing which our language can boaſt.

In 1750 he put his finiſhing ſtroke to his *Elegy written in a Country Church-yard*, which was communicated firſt to his friend Mr. Walpole, and by him to many perſons of rank and diſtinction. This beautiful production introduced the author to the favour of Lady Cobham, and gave occaſion to a ſingular compoſition, fition, called, *A Long Story*; in which various effufions of wit and humour are very happily interfperfed.

The Elegy having found its way into the "Magazine of Magazines," the Author wrote to Mr. Walpole, requefting he would put it into the hands of Mr. Dodfley, and order him to print it immediately, in order to refcue it from the difgrace it might have incurred by its appearance in a Magazine. The Elegy was the moft popular of all our Author's productions; it ran through eleven editions, and was tranflated into Latin by Anftey and Roberts; and in the fame year a verfion of it was publifhed by Lloyd. Mr. Bentley, an eminent Artift of that time, wifhing to decorate this elegant compofition with every ornament of which it is fo highly deferving, drew for it a fet of defigns, as he alfo did for the reft of Gray's productions, for which the artift was liberally repaid by the Author in fome beautiful Stanzas, but unfortunately no perfect copy of them remains. The following, however, are given as a fpecimen:

" In filent gaze the tuneful choir among,
" Half pleas'd, half blufhing, let the mufe admire,
" While Bentley leads her fifter art along,
" And bids the pencil anfwer to the lyre.

" See, in their courfe, each tranfitory thought,
" Fix'd by his touch, a lafting effence take;
" Each dream, in fancy's airy colouring wrought,
" To local fymmetry and life awake!

" The tardy rhymes, that us'd to linger on,
" To cenfure cold, and negligent of fame;
" In fwifter meafures animated run,
" And catch a luftre from his genuine flame.

" Ah! could they catch his ftrength, his eafy grace,
" His quick creation, his unerring line;
" The energy of Pope they might efface,
" And Dryden's harmony fubmit to mine.

" But not to one in this benighted age
" Is that diviner infpiration giv'n,
" That burns in Shakefpear's or in Milton's page,
" The pomp and prodigality of heav'n,

"As when conspiring in the di'mond's blaze,
"The meaner gems, that singly charm the sight,
"Together dart their intermingled rays,
"And dazzle with a luxury of light.

"Enough for me, if to some feeling breast
"My lines a secret sympathy impart,
"And, as their pleasing influence flows confess'd,
"A sigh of soft reflection heave the heart."

It appears, by a letter to Dr. Wharton, that Gray finished his Ode on the *Progress of Poetry* early in 1755. The *Bard* also was begun about the same time; and the following beautiful Fragment on the *Pleasure arising from Vicissitude* the next year. The merit of the two former pieces was not immediately perceived, nor generally acknowledged. Garrick wrote a few lines in their praise. Lloyd and Colman wrote, in concert, two Odes to "Oblivion" and "Obscurity," in which they were ridiculed with much ingenuity.

"Now the golden morn aloft
"Waves her dew-bespangled wing,
"With vermil cheek, and whisper soft,
"She wooes the tardy spring;
"Till April starts, and calls around
"The sleeping fragrance from the ground,
"And lightly o'er the living scene
"Scatters his freshest, tenderest green.

"New-born flocks, in rustic dance,
"Frisking ply their feeble feet;
"Forgetful of their wint'ry trance,
"The birds his presence greet:
"But chief the skylark warbles high
"His trembling, thrilling extacy;
"And, lessening from the dazzled sight,
"Melts into air and liquid light.

"Yesterday the sullen year
"Saw the snowy whirlwind fly;
"Mute was the music of the air,
"The herd stood drooping by:
"Their raptures now, that wildly flow,
"No yesterday nor morrow know;
"'Tis man alone that joy descries
"With forward and reverted eyes.

"Smiles on past misfortune's brow
"Soft reflection's hand can trace,
"And o'er the cheek of sorrow throw
"A melancholy grace;

"While

"While hope prolongs our happier hour;
"Or deepest shades, that dimly lower,
"And blacken round our weary way,
"Gilds with a gleam of distant day.

"Still where rosy pleasure leads,
"See a kindred grief pursue,
"Behind the steps that misery treads
"Approaching comfort view:
"The hues of bliss more brightly glow,
"Chastiz'd by sabler tints of woe;
"And blended form, with artful strife,
"The strength and harmony of life.

"See the wretch, that long has tost
"On the thorny bed of Pain,
"At length repair his vigour lost,
"And breathe and walk again.
"The meanest flow'ret of the vale,
"The simplest note that swells the gale,
"The common sun, the air, the skies,
"To him are opening Paradise."

Our Author's reputation, as a Poet, was so high, that, on the death of Colley Cibber, in 1757, he had the honour of refusing the office of Poet-Laureat, to which he was probably induced by the disgrace brought upon it through the inability of some who had filled it.

His curiosity some time after drew him away from Cambridge to a lodging near the British Museum, where he resided near three years, reading and transcribing.

In 1762, on the death of Mr. Turner, Professor of Modern Languages and History at Cambridge, he was, according to his own expression, "cockered and spirited up" to apply to Lord Bute for the succession. His Lordship refused him with all the politeness of a courtier, the office having been previously promised to Mr. Brocket, the tutor of Sir James Lowther.

His health being on the decline, in 1765 he undertook a journey to Scotland, conceiving he should derive benefit from exercise and change of situation. His account of that country, as far as it extends, is curious and elegant; for as his mind was comprehensive, it was employed in the contemplation of all the works of art, all the appearances of nature, and all the monuments of past events.

During his stay in Scotland, he contracted a friendship with Dr. Beattie, in whom he found, as he himself expresses it, a poet, a philosopher, and a good man. Through the intervention of his friend the Doctor, the Marischal College at Aberdeen offered him the degree of Doctor of Laws, which he thought it decent to decline, having omitted to take it at Cambridge.

In December, 1767, Dr. Beattie, still desirous that his country should leave a memento of its regard to the merit of our Poet, solicited his permission to print, at the University of Glasgow, an elegant edition of his works. Gray could not comply with his friend's request, as he had given his promise to Mr. Dodsley. However, as a compliment to them both, he presented them with a copy, containing a few notes, and the imitations of the old Norwegian poetry, intended to supplant the Long Story, which was printed at first to illustrate Mr. Bentley's designs.

In 1768 our Author obtained that office without solicitation, for which he had before applied without effect. The Professorship of Languages and History again became vacant, and he received an offer of it from the Duke of Grafton, who had succeeded Lord Bute in office. The place was valuable in itself, the salary being 400l. a year; but it was rendered peculiarly acceptable to Mr. Gray, as he obtained it without solicitation.

Soon after he succeeded to this office, the impaired state of his health rendered another journey necessary; and he visited, in 1769, the counties of Westmoreland and Cumberland. His remarks on the wonderful scenery which these northern regions display, he transmitted in epistolary journals to his friend, Dr. Wharton, which abound, according to Mr. Mason's elegant diction,

diction, with all the wildness of Salvator, and the softness of Claude.

He appears to have been much affected by the anxiety he felt at holding a place without discharging the duties annexed to it. He had always designed reading lectures, but never put it in practice; and a consciousness of this neglect contributed not a little to increase the malady under which he had long laboured: nay, the office at length became so irksome, that he seriously proposed to resign it.

Towards the close of May, 1771, he removed from Cambridge to London, after having suffered violent attacks of an hereditary gout, to which he had long been subject, notwithstanding he had observed the most rigid abstemiousness throughout the whole course of his life. By the advice of his physicians, he removed from London to Kensington; the air of which place proved so salutary, that he was soon enabled to return to Cambridge, whence he designed to make a visit to his friend Dr. Wharton, at Old Park, near Durham; indulging a fond hope that the excursion would tend to the re-establishment of his health: but, alas! that hope proved delusive. On the 24th of July he was seized, while at dinner in the College hall, with a sudden nausea, which obliged him to retire to his chamber. The gout had fixed on his stomach in such a degree as to resist all the powers of medicine. On the 29th he was attacked with a strong convulsion, which returned with increased violence the ensuing day; and on the evening of the 31st of May, 1771, he departed this life in the 55th year of his age.

From the narrative of his friend, Mr. Mason, it appears, that Gray was actuated by motives of self improvement, and self gratification, in his application to the Muses, rather than any view to pecuniary emolument. His pursuits were in general disinterested; and as he was free from avarice on the one hand, so was he from extravagance on the other; being one of
those

those few characters in the annals of literature, especially in the poetical class, who are devoid of self interest, and at the same time attentive to economy; but Mr. Mason adds, that he was induced to decline taking any advantage of his literary productions by a degree of pride, which influenced him to disdain the idea of being thought an author by profession.

It appears, from the same narrative, that Gray made considerable progress in the study of architecture, particularly the gothic. He endeavoured to trace this branch of the science, from the period of its commencement, through its various changes, till it arrived at its perfection in the time of Henry VIII. He applied himself also to the study of heraldry, of which he obtained a very competent knowledge, as appears from his *Remarks on Saxon Churches*, in the introduction to Mr. Bentham's *History of Ely*.

But the favourite study of Gray, for the last two years of his life, was natural history, which he rather resumed than began, as he had acquired some knowledge of botany in early life, while he was under the tuition of his uncle Antrobus. He wrote copious marginal notes to the works of Linnæus, and other writers in the three kingdoms of nature: and Mr. Mason further observes, that, excepting pure mathematics, and the studies dependent on that science, there was hardly any part of human learning in which he had not acquired a competent skill; in most of them a consummate mastery.

Mr. Mason has declined drawing any formal character of him; but has adopted one from a letter to James Boswell, Esq. by the Rev. Mr. Temple, Rector of St. Gluvias, in Cornwall, first printed anonymously in the London Magazine, which, as we conceive authentic, from the sanction of Mr. Mason, we shall therefore transcribe.

" Perhaps he was the most learned man in Europe. He was equally acquainted with the elegant and profound parts of science, and that not superficially, but
                                             thoroughly.

thoroughly. He knew every branch of history, both natural and civil; had read all the original historians of England, France, and Italy; and was a great antiquarian. Criticism, metaphysics, morals, and politics, made a principal part of his study; voyages and travels of all sorts were his favourite amusements; and he had a fine taste in painting, prints, architecture, and gardening. With such a fund of knowledge, his conversation must have been equally instructive and entertaining; but he was also a good man, a man of virtue and humanity. There is no character without some speck, some imperfection; and I think the greatest defect in his was an affectation in delicacy, or rather effeminacy, and a visible fastidiousness, or contempt and disdain of his inferiors in science. He also had, in some degree, that weakness which disgusted Voltaire so much in Mr. Congreve: though he seemed to value others chiefly according to the progress they had made in knowledge, yet he could not bear to be considered himself merely as a man of letters; and though without birth, or fortune, or station, his desire was to be looked upon as a private independent gentleman, who read for his amusement. Perhaps it may be said, What signifies so much knowledge, when it produced so little? Is it worth taking so much pains to leave no memorial but a few Poems? But let it be considered that Mr. Gray was, to others, at least innocently employed; to himself, certainly beneficially. His time passed agreeably; he was every day making some new acquisition in science; his mind was enlarged, his heart softened, his virtue strengthened; the world and mankind were shewn to him without a mask; and he was taught to consider every thing as trifling, and unworthy of the attention of a wise man, except the pursuit of knowledge and practice of virtue, in that state wherein God hath placed us."

In addition to this character, Mr. Mason has remarked, that Gray's effeminacy was affected most

before

before those whom he did not wish to please; and that he is unjustly charged with making knowledge his sole reason of preference, as he paid his esteem to none whom he did not likewise believe to be good.

Dr. Johnson makes the following observations:—
"What has occurred to me, from the slight inspection of his letters, in which my undertaking has engaged me, is, that his mind had a large grasp; that his curiosity was unlimited, and his judgment cultivated; that he was a man likely to love much where he loved at all, but that he was fastidious, and hard to please. His contempt, however, is often employed, where I hope it will be approved, upon scepticism and infidelity. His short account of Shaftesbury I will insert.

"You say you cannot conceive how lord Shaftesbury came to be a philosopher in vogue; I will tell you: first, he was a lord; secondly, he was as vain as any of his readers; thirdly, men are very prone to believe what they do not understand; fourthly, they will believe any thing at all, provided they are under no obligation to believe it; fifthly, they love to take a new road, even when that road leads no where; sixthly, he was reckoned a fine writer, and seems always to mean more than he said. Would you have any more reasons? An interval of above forty years has pretty well destroyed the charm. A dead lord ranks with commoners: vanity is no longer interested in the matter; for a new road is become an old one."

As a writer he had this peculiarity, that he did not write his pieces first rudely, and then correct them, but laboured every line as it arose in the train of composition; and he had a notion not very peculiar, that he could not write but at certain times, or at happy moments; a fantastic foppery, to which our kindness for a man of learning and of virtue wishes him to have been superior.

As a Poet he stands high in the estimation of the candid and judicious. His works are not numerous;
but

but they bear the marks of intense application, and careful revision. The Elegy in the Churchyard is deemed his master-piece; the subject is interesting, the sentiment simple and pathetic, and the versification charmingly melodious. This beautiful composition has been often selected by orators for the display of their rhetorical talents. But as the most finished productions of the human mind have not escaped censure, the works of our Author have undergone illiberal comments. His Elegy has been supposed defective in want of plan. Dr. Knox, in his Essays, has observed, " that it is thought by some to be no more than a confused heap of splendid ideas, thrown together without order and without proportion." Some passages have been censured by Kelly in the *Babbler*; and imitations of different authors have been pointed out by other critics. But these imitations cannot be ascertained, as there are numberless instances of coincidence of ideas; so that it is difficult to say, with precision, what is or is not a designed or accidental imitation.

Gray, in his Elegy in the Church-yard, has great merit in adverting to the most interesting passions of the human mind; yet his genius is not marked alone by the tender sensibility so conspicuous in that elegant piece; but there is a sublimity which gives it an equal claim to universal admiration.

His Odes on *The Progress of Poetry*, and of *The Bard*, according to Mr. Mason's account, " breathe the high spirit of lyric enthusiasm. The transitions are sudden and impetuous; the language full of fire and force; and the imagery carried, without impropriety, to the most daring height. They have been accused of obscurity: but the one can be obscure to those only who have not read Pindar; and the other only to those who are unacquainted with the history of our own nation."

Of his other lyric pieces, Mr. Wakefield, a learned and ingenious commentator, observes, that, though, like

like all other human productions, they are not without their defects, yet the spirit of poetry, and exquisite charms of the verse, are more then a compensation for those defects. The Ode on *Eton College* abounds with sentiments natural, and consonant to the feelings of humanity, exhibited with perspicuity of method, and in elegant, intelligible, and expressive language. The Sonnet on *the Death of West*, and the Epitaph on *Sir William Williams*, are as perfect compositions of the kind as any in our language.

Dr. Johnson was confessedly a man of great genius; but the partial and uncandid mode of criticism he has adopted in his remarks on the writings of Gray, has given to liberal minds great and just offence. According to Mr. Mason's account, he has subjected Gray's poetry to the most rigorous examination. Declining all consideration of the general plan and conduct of the pieces, he has confined himself solely to strictures on words and forms of expression; and Mr. Mason very pertinently adds, that *verbal* criticism is an ordeal which the most perfect composition cannot pass without injury.

He has also fallen under Mr. Wakefield's severest censure. This commentator affirms, that "he thinks a refutation of his strictures upon Gray a necessary service to the public, without which they might operate with a malignant influence upon the national taste. His censure, however, is too general, and expressed with too much vehemence; and his remarks betray, upon the whole, an unreasonable fastidiousness of taste, and an unbecoming illiberality of spirit. He appears to have turned an unwilling eye upon the beauties of Gray, because his jealousy would not suffer him to see such superlative merit in a cotemporary." These remarks of Mr. Wakefield appear to be well founded; and it has been observed, by another writer, that Dr. Johnson, being strongly influenced by his political and religious principles, was inclined to treat with

the

the utmost severity some of the productions of our best writers; to which may be imputed that severity with which he censures the lyric performances of Gray. It is highly probable that no one poetical reader will universally subscribe to his decisions, though all may admire his vast intuitive knowledge, and power of discrimination.

In the first copy of this exquisite Poem, Mr. Mason observes, the conclusion was different from that which the Author afterwards composed; and though his after-thought was unquestionably the best, yet there is a pathetic melancholy in the four stanzas that were rejected, following, "With incense kindled at the Muses' flame," which highly claim preservation.

> The thoughtless world to Majesty may bow,
> Exalt the brave, and idolize success;
> But more to innocence their safety owe,
> Than pow'r or genius e'er conspir'd to bless.
>
> And thou who, mindful of th' unhonour'd dead,
> Dost in these notes their artless tale relate,
> By night and lonely contemplation led,
> To wander in the gloomy walks of fate,
>
> Hark! how the sacred calm, that breathes around,
> Bids every fierce tumultuous passion cease;
> In still small accents whispering from the ground,
> A grateful earnest of eternal peace.
>
> No more, with reason and thyself at strife,
> Give anxious cares and endless wishes room;
> But, through the cool sequester'd vale of life,
> Pursue the silent tenor of thy doom.

In one instance, the Doctor's inconsistency, and deviation from his general character, does him honour. After having commented with the most rigid severity on the poetical works of Gray, as if conscious of the injustice done him, he seems to apologize by the following declaration, which concludes his Criticism, and shall conclude the Memoirs of our Author.

"In the character of his Elegy (says Johnson) I rejoice and concur with the common reader; for, by the common sense of readers, uncorrupted with literary prejudices,

prejudices, after all the refinements of subtilty, and the dogmatism of learning, must be finally decided all claim to poetical honours. The *Church-yard* abounds with images which find a mirror in every mind, and with sentiments to which every bosom returns an echo. The four stanzas beginning, *Yet e'en these bones* are to me original; I have never seen the notions in any other place; yet he that reads them here, persuades himself that he has always felt them. Had Gray written often thus, it had been vain to blame, and useless to praise him."

THE TEARS OF GENIUS,

AN ODE,

TO THE MEMORY OF MR. GRAY.

(By J. T--------.)

ON Cham's fair banks, where Learning's hallow'd fane
    Majestic rises on th' astonish'd sight,
Where oft the Muse has led the fav'rite swain,
And warm'd his soul with heav'n's inspiring light;

Beneath the covert of the sylvan shade,
Where deadly cypress, mix'd with mournful yew,
Far o'er the vale a gloomy stillness spread,
Celestial Genius burst upon the view.

The bloom of youth, the majesty of years,
The soften'd aspect, innocent and kind,
The sigh of sorrow, and the streaming tears,
Resistless all, their various pow'r combin'd.

In her fair hand a silver harp she bore,
Whose magic notes, soft warbling from the string,
Give tranquil joys the breast ne'er knew before,
Or raise the soul on rapture's airy wing.
By grief impell'd, I heard her heave a sigh,
While thus the rapid strain resounded thro' the sky:

Haste ye sister pow'rs of Song!
Hasten from the shady grove,
Where the river rolls along
Sweetly to the voice of love;

Where, indulging mirthful pleasures,
Light you press the flow'ry green,
And from Flora's blooming treasures
Cull the wreath for Fancy's queen;

Where your gently-flowing numbers,
Floating on the fragrant breeze,
Sink the soul in pleasing slumbers
On the downy bed of ease.

For graver strains prepare the plaintive lyre,
That wakes the softest feelings of the soul;
Let lonely grief the melting verse inspire,
Let deep'ning sorrow's solemn accents roll.

Rack'd by the hand of rude Disease,
Behold our fav'rite Poet lies!
While ev'ry object form'd to please
Far from his couch ungrateful flies.

The blissful Muse, whose fav'ring smile
So lately warm'd his peaceful breast,
Diffusing heav'nly joys the while,
In Transport's radiant garments drest,
With darksome grandeur, and enfeebled blaze,
Sinks in the shades of night, and shuns his eager gaze.

The gaudy train who wait on Spring,*
Ting'd with the pomp of vernal pride,
The youth, who mount on pleasure's wing,†
And idly sport on Thames's side,
With cool regard their various arts employ,
Nor rouse the drooping mind, nor give the pause of joy.

Ha! what forms, with port sublime,§
Glide along in sullen mood,
Scorning all the threats of time,
High above misfortune's flood!

They seize their harps, they strike the lyre,
With rapid hand, with freedom's fire;
Obedient Nature hears the lofty sound,
And Snowdon's airy cliffs the heavenly strains resound.

In pomp of state behold they wait,
With arms outstretch'd and aspects kind,
To snatch on high to yonder sky
The child of Fancy left behind;
Forgot the woes of Cambria's fatal day,
By rapture's blaze impell'd, they swell the artless lay.

But, ah! in vain they strive to sooth
With gentle arts the tort'ring hours.
Adversity ‡ with rankling tooth
Her baleful gifts profusely pours.

Behold she comes! the fiend forlorn,
Array'd in Horrour's settled gloom;
She strews the brier and prickly thorn,
And triumphs in th' infernal doom;
With frantic fury, and insatiate rage, [page.
She gnaws the throbbing breast, and blasts the glowing

No more the soft Eolian flute‖
Breathes thro' the heart the melting strain,
The pow'rs of Harmony are mute,
And leave the once-delightful plain;
With heavy wing I see them beat the air,
Damp'd by the leaden hand of comfortless Despair.

C   Yet

* Ode on Spring.   † Ode on the Prospect of Eton College.
§ Bard, an Ode.   ‡ Ode to Adversity.   ‖ The Progress of Poetry.

Yet stay, O stay! celestial Pow'rs!
And with a hand of kind regard
Dispel the boist'rous storm that lours
Destructive on the fav'rite bard;
O watch with me his last expiring breath,
And snatch him from the arms of dark oblivious Death!

Hark! the Fatal Sisters ‡ join,
And, with horrour's mutt'ring sounds,
Weave the tissue of his line,
While the dreadful spell resounds,

" Hail, ye midnight Sisters! hail!
" Drive the shuttle swift along,
" Let our secret charms prevail
" O'er the valiant and the strong;

" O'er the glory of the land,
" O'er the innocent and gay,
" O'er the Muses' tuneful band,
" Weave the fun'ral web of Gray."

'Tis done, 'tis done---the iron hand of Pain,
With ruthless fury and corrosive force,
Racks ev'ry joint, and seizes ev'ry vein:
He sinks, he groans, he falls, a lifeless corse!

Thus fades the flow'r, nipp'd by the frozen gale,
Tho' once so sweet, so lovely to the eye;
Thus the tall oaks, when boist'rous storms assail,
Torn from the earth, a mighty ruin lie.

Ye sacred Sisters of the plaintive verse,
Now let the stream of fond affection flow;
O pay your tribute o'er the slow-drawn hearse
With all the manly dignity of woe!

Oft' when the curfew tolls its parting knell,
With solemn pause yon' Churchyard's gloom survey,
While sorrow's sighs and tears of pity tell
How just the moral of the poet's lay. *

O'er his green grave, in Contemplation's guise,
Oft' let the pilgrim drop a silent tear,
Oft' let the shepherd's tender accents rise,
Big with the sweets of each revolving year,
Till prostrate Time adore his deathless name,
Fix'd on the solid base of adamantine fame.

‡ The Fatal Sisters, an Ode.
* Elegy in a Country Churchyard.

ODES.

ODE I.
ON THE SPRING.

LO! where the rosy-bosom'd hours,
   Fair Venus' train, appear,
Disclose the long-expecting flow'rs,
   And wake the purple year,
The attic warbler pours her throat   5
Responsive to the cuckoo's note,
The untaught harmony of spring,
While, whisp'ring pleasure as they fly,
Cool zephyrs thro' the clear blue sky
   Their gather'd fragrance fling.   10

Where'er the oak's thick branches stretch
   A broader, browner shade,
Where'er the rude and moss-grown beech
   O'er-canopies the glade,*
Beside some water's rushy brink   15
With me the Muse shall sit, and think
   (At ease reclin'd in rustic state)
How vain the ardour of the crowd,
How low, how little, are the proud,
   How indigent the great!   20

Still is the toiling hand of Care,
   The panting herds repose,
Yet hark! how thro' the peopled air
   The busy murmur glows!
The insect youth are on the wing,   25
Eager to taste the honey'd spring,

---

* ------------------------a bank
O'er-canopy'd with luscious woodbine.
       Shakesp. Mid. Night's Dream.

And float amid the liquid noon;*
Some lightly o'er the current skim,
Some shew their gayly-gilded trim,
Quick-glancing to the sun.†   30

To contemplation's sober eye,‡
Such is the race of man,
And they that creep, and they that fly,
Shall end where they began.
Alike the busy and the gay   35
But flutter thro' life's little day,
In Fortune's varying colours drest;
Brush'd by the hand of rough Mischance,
Or chill'd by Age, their airy dance
They leave, in dust to rest.   40

Methinks I hear, in accents low,
The sportive kind reply,
Poor Moralist! and what art thou?
A solitary fly!
Thy joys no glitt'ring female meets,   45
No hive hast thou of hoarded sweets,
No painted plumage to display;
On hasty wings thy youth is flown,
Thy sun is set, thy spring is gone—
We frolic while 'tis May.   50

ODE II.
ON THE
DEATH OF A FAVOURITE CAT,
Drowned in a Tub of Gold Fishes.

'TWAS on a lofty vase's side,
  Where China's gayest art had dy'd
The azure flowers that blow,
Demurest of the tabby kind,
The pensive Selima, reclin'd,
  Gaz'd on the lake below.   6

---
* Nare per æstatem liquidam.   *Virg. Georg. lib.* 4
† ———— ———— sporting with quick glance,
  Shew to the sun their wav'd coats dropt with gold.
                          Milton's Paradise Lost, b. 7.
‡ While insects from the threshold preach, &c.
Mr. *Green in the Grotto.* Dodsley's *Miscellanies, vol.* v. *p.* 161.

Her conscious tail her joy declar'd;
The fair round face, the snowy beard,
The velvet of her paws,
Her coat that with the tortoise vies,
Her ears of jet, and em'rald eyes,
She saw, and purr'd applause.

Still had she gaz'd, but, 'midst the tide,
Two angel forms were seen to glide,
The Genii of the stream;
Their scaly armour's Tyrian hue,
Thro' richest purple, to the view
Betray'd a golden gleam.

The hapless nymph with wonder saw:
A whisker first, and then a claw,
With many an ardent wish,
She stretch'd in vain to reach the prize:
What female heart can gold despise?
What Cat's averse to fish?

Presumpt'ous maid! with looks intent,
Again she stretch'd, again she bent,
Nor knew the gulf between:
(Malignant Fate sat by and smil'd,)
The slipp'ry verge her feet beguil'd;
She tumbled headlong in.

Eight times emerging from the flood,
She mew'd to ev'ry wat'ry god
Some speedy aid to send.
No Dolphin came, no Nereid stirr'd,
Nor cruel Tom or Susan heard:
A fav'rite has no friend!

From hence, ye Beauties! undeceiv'd,
Know one false step is ne'er retriev'd,
And be with caution bold:
Not all that tempts your wand'ring eyes,
And heedless hearts, is lawful prize,
Nor all that glisters gold.

ODE III.

ON A
DISTANT PROSPECT OF ETON COLLEGE.

'Ανθρωπος· ἱκανὴ πρόφασις εἰς τὸ δυςυχεῖν.   *Menander.*

YE diſtant Spires! ye antique Tow'rs!
That crown the watry glade
Where grateful Science ſtill adores
Her Henry's * holy ſhade;
And ye that from the ſtately brow   5
Of Windſor's heights th' expanſe below
Of grove, of lawn, of mead, ſurvey,
Whoſe turf, whoſe ſhade, whoſe flow'rs, among
Wanders the hoary Thames along
His ſilver-winding way: 10

Ah happy hills! ah pleaſing ſhade!
Ah fields belov'd in vain!
Where once my careleſs childhood ſtray'd,
A ſtranger yet to pain!
I feel the gales that from ye blow   15
A momentary bliſs beſtow,
As waving freſh their gladſome wing
My weary ſoul they ſeem to ſooth,
And, redolent † of joy and youth,
To breathe a ſecond ſpring.   20

Say, father Thames! for thou haſt ſeen
Full many a ſprightly race,
Diſporting on thy margent green,
The paths of pleaſure trace,
Who foremoſt now delight to cleave   25
With pliant arm thy glaſſy wave?
The captive linnet which enthral?
What idle progeny ſucceed
To chaſe the rolling circle's ſpeed,
Or urge the flying ball?   30

* King Henry VI. founder of the College.
† And bees their honey redolent of ſpring.
   Dryden's Fable on the Pythag. Syſtem.

While some, on earnest bus'ness bent,
Their murm'ring labours ply
'Gainst graver hours, that bring constraint,
To sweeten liberty;
Some bold adventurers disdain
The limits of their little reign,
And unknown regions dare descry;
Still as they run they look behind,
They hear a voice in ev'ry wind,
And snatch a fearful joy.

Gay hope is theirs, by fancy fed,
Less pleasing when possest;
The tear forgot as soon as shed,
The sunshine of the breast;
Theirs buxom health of rosy hue,
Wild wit, invention ever new,
And lively cheer of vigour born;
The thoughtless day, the easy night,
The spirits pure, the slumbers light,
That fly th' approach of morn.

Alas! regardless of their doom,
The little victims play!
No sense have they of ills to come,
Nor care beyond to day:
Yet see how all around 'em wait
The ministers of human fate,
And black Misfortune's baleful train!
Ah! shew them where in ambush stand,
To seize their prey, the murd'rous band!
Ah! tell them they are men.

These shall the fury Passions tear,
The vultures of the mind,
Disdainful Anger, pallid Fear,
And Shame that sculks behind;
Or pining Love shall waste their youth,
Or Jealousy, with rankling tooth,

That inly gnaws the secret heart;
And Envy wan, and faded Care,
Grim-visag'd, comfortless Despair,
And Sorrow's piercing dart. 70

Ambition this shall tempt to rise,
Then whirl the wretch from high,
To bitter Scorn a sacrifice,
And grinning Infamy:
The stings of Falsehood those shall try, 75
And hard Unkindness' alter'd eye,
That mocks the tear it forc'd to flow;
And keen Remorse, with blood defil'd,
And moody Madness * laughing wild
Amid severest woe. 80

Lo! in the vale of years beneath
A grisly troop are seen,
The painful family of Death,
More hideous than their queen:
This racks the joints, this fires the veins, 85
That ev'ry lab'ring sinew strains,
Those in the deeper vitals rage;
Lo! Poverty, to fill the band,
That numbs the soul with icy hand,
And slow-consuming Age. 90

To each his suff'rings; all are men
Condemn'd alike to groan;
The tender for another's pain,
Th' unfeeling for his own.
Yet ah! why should they know their fate, 95
Since sorrow never comes too late,
And happiness too swiftly flies?
Thought would destroy their paradise.
No more; where ignorance is bliss
'Tis folly to be wise. 100

* And Madness laughing in his ireful mood.
    Dryden's Fable of Palamon and Arcite.

ODE IV.
TO ADVERSITY.

--------- Ζῆνα
Τὸν φρονεῖν βροτοὺς ὁδώ-
σαντα, τῶι πάθει μάθὼν
Θέντα κυρίως ἔχειν.
Aeschylus in Agamemnone.

DAUGHTER of Jove, relentless pow'r,
   Thou tamer of the human breast,
Whose iron scourge and tort'ring hour
The bad affright, afflict the best!
Bound in thy adamantine chain,   5
The proud are taught to taste of pain,
And purple tyrants vainly groan
With pangs unfelt before, unpity'd and alone.

When first thy sire to send on earth
Virtue, his darling child, design'd,   10
To thee he gave the heav'nly birth,
And bad to form her infant mind;
Stern rugged nurse! thy rigid lore
With patience many a year she bore;
What sorrow was thou bad'st her know,   15
And from her own she learn'd to melt at others' woe.

Scar'd at thy frown terrific fly
Self-pleasing Folly's idle brood,
Wild Laughter, Noise, and thoughtless Joy,
And leave us leisure to be good.   20
Light they disperse; and with them go
The summer friend, the flatt'ring foe;
By vain Prosperity receiv'd,
To her they vow their truth, and are again believ'd.

Wisdom, in sable garb array'd,   25
Immers'd in rapt'rous thought profound,
And Melancholy, silent maid,
With leaden eye, that loves the ground,

Still on thy solemn steps attend;
Warm Charity, the gen'ral friend,
With Justice, to herself severe,
And Pity, dropping soft the sadly-pleasing tear.

Oh! gently on thy suppliant's head,
Dread goddess! lay thy chast'ning hand,
Not in thy Gorgon terrours clad,
Nor circled with the vengeful band:
(As by the impious thou art seen,)
With thund'ring voice and threatning mien,
With screaming Horrour's fun'ral cry,
Despair, and fell Disease, and ghastly Poverty.

Thy form benign, O Goddess! wear,
Thy milder influence impart,
Thy philosophic train be there,
To soften, not to wound, my heart;
The gen'rous spark extinct revive;
Teach me to love and to forgive;
Exact my own defects to scan,
What others are to feel, and know myself a man.

ODE V.

THE PROGRESS OF POESY.

PINDARICK.

Advertisement.

WHEN the Author first published this and the following Ode, he was advised, even by his Friends, to subjoin some few explanatory Notes, but had too much respect for the Understanding of his Readers to take that Liberty.

Φωνᾶντα συνετοῖσιν' ἐς
Δὲ τὸ πᾶν ἑρμηνέων
Χατίζει.............
   Pindar, Olymp. ii.

I. 1.

AWAKE, Æolian lyre! awake,*
 And give to rapture all thy trembling strings;
From Helicon's harmonious springs
A thousand rills their mazy progress take;
The laughing flow'rs, that round them blow,   5
Drink life and fragrance as they flow.
Now the rich stream of musick winds along
Deep, majestic, smooth, and strong,
Thro' verdant vales and Ceres' golden reign;
Now rolling down the steep amain,   10
Headlong, impetuous, see it pour;
The rocks and nodding groves rebellow to the roar.

I. 2.

Oh! Sov'reign† of the willing soul,
Parent of sweet and solemn-breathing airs,
Enchanting shell! the sullen Cares   15
And frantic Passions hear thy soft controul.

---

* Awake, my glory! awake, lute and harp.
        David's Psalms.
Pindar styles his own poetry, with its musical accompaniments, Αἰολῃὶς μολπὴ, Αἰολίδες χορδαὶ, Αἰολίδων πνοαὶ αὐλῶν. Æolian song, Æolian strings, the breath of the Æolian flute. The subject and simile, as usual with Pindar, are here united. The various sources of poetry, which gives life and lustre to all it touches, are here described, as well in its quiet majestic progress, enriching every subject (otherwise dry and barren) with all the pomp of diction, and luxuriant harmony of numbers, as in its more rapid and irresistible course, when swoln and hurried away by the conflict of tumultuous passions.

† Power of harmony to calm the turbulent passions of the soul. The thoughts are borrowed from the first Pythian of Pindar.

On Thracia's hills the Lord of War
Has curb'd the fury of his car,
And dropp'd his thirsty lance at thy command:
Perching on the sceptred hand† 20
Of Jove, thy magic lulls the feather'd king
With ruffled plumes and flagging wing;
Quench'd in dark clouds of slumber lie
The terrour of his beak and lightnings of his eye.

I. 3.

Thee ‡ the voice, the dance obey, 25
Temper'd to thy warbled lay:
O'er Idalia's velvet green
The rosy-crowned Loves are seen,
On Cytherea's day,
With antic Sports and blue-ey'd Pleasures 30
Frisking light in frolic measures:
Now pursuing, now retreating,
Now in circling troops they meet;
To brisk notes in cadence beating,
Glance their many-twinkling feet.§ 35
Slow-melting strains their queen's approach declare;
Where'er she turns the Graces homage pay;
With arms sublime, that float upon the air,
In gliding state she wins her easy way:
O'er her warm cheek and rising bosom move 40
The bloom of young desire and purple light of love.‖

II. 1.

Man's feeble race what ills await!¶
Labour and Penury, the racks of Pain,
Disease, and Sorrow's weeping train,
And Death, sad refuge from the storms of Fate! 45

---

† This is a weak imitation of some beautiful lines in the same ode.
‡ Power of harmony to produce all the graces of motion in the body.
§ Μαρμαρυγὰς θηεῖτο ποδῶν· θαύμαζε δὲ θυμῷ.
                              Homer, Od. Θ.
‖ Λάμπει δ' ἐπὶ πορφυρέῃσι.
  Παρείῃσι φᾶς ἔρωτος.   Phrynichus apud Athenæum.
¶ To compensate the real or imaginary ills of Life, the Muse was given to mankind by the same Providence that lends the day by its cheerful presence to dispel the gloom and terrours of the night.

The fond complaint, my Song! disprove,
And justify the laws of Jove.
Say, has he giv'n in vain the heav'nly Muse?
Night and all her sickly dews,
Her spectres wan, and birds of boding cry, 50
He gives to range the dreary sky,
Till down the eastern cliffs afar †
Hyperion's march they spy and glitt'ring shafts of war.

II. 2.

In climes ‡ beyond the Solar Road, §
Where shaggy forms o'er ice-built mountains roam,
The Muse has broke the twilight-gloom 56
To cheer the shiv'ring native's dull abode:
And oft' beneath the od'rous shade
Of Chili's boundless forests laid,
She deigns to hear the savage youth repeat, 60
In loose numbers, wildly sweet,
Their feather-cinctur'd chiefs and dusky loves.
Her track, where'er the goddess roves,
Glory pursue, and gen'rous shame,
Th' unconquerable mind and freedom's holy flame. 65

II. 3.

Woods that wave o'er Delphia's steep, ‖
Isles that crown th' Ægian deep,
Fields that cool Ilissus laves,
Or where Mæander's amber waves
In ling'ring lab'rinths creep, 70

---

† Or seen the morning's well-appointed star
Come marching up the eastern hills afar. *Cowley.*

‡ Extensive influence of poetic genius over the remotest and most uncivilized nations; its connection with liberty, and the virtues that naturally attend on it. [See the Erse, Norwegian, and Welsh Fragments, the Lapland and American Songs, &c.]

§ Extra anni solisque vias.——— *Virgil.*
Tutta lontana dal camin del sole. *Petrarch. Canz.* 2.

‖ Progress of Poetry from Greece to Italy, and from Italy to England. Chaucer was not unacquainted with the writings of Dante or of Petrarch. The Earl of Surrey and Sir Thomas Wyatt had travelled in Italy, and formed their taste there: Spencer imitated the Italian writers, Milton improved on them: but this school expired soon after the Restoration, and a new one arose, on the French model, which has subsisted ever since.

How do your tuneful echoes languish,
Mute but to the voice of Anguish?
Where each old poetic mountain
Inspiration breath'd around,
Ev'ry shade and hallow'd fountain 75
Murmur'd deep a solemn sound,
Till the sad Nine, in Greece's evil hour,
Left their Parnassus for the Latian plains:
Alike they scorn the pomp of tyrant Pow'r
And coward Vice, that revels in her chains. 80
When Latium had her lofty spirit lost,
They sought, oh Albion! next thy sea-encircled coast.

III. 1.

Far from the sun and summer-gale,
In thy green lap was Nature's darling † laid,
What time, where lucid Avon stray'd, 85
To him the mighty Mother did unveil
Her awful face: the dauntless child
Stretch'd forth his little arms, and smil'd.
This pencil take (she said) whose colours clear
Richly paint the vernal year; 90
Thine too these golden keys, immortal boy!
This can unlock the gates of Joy,
Of Horror that, and thrilling Fears,
Or ope the sacred source of sympathetic Tears.

III. 2.

Nor second he ‡ that rode sublime 95
Upon the seraph-wings of Ecstacy,
The secrets of th' abyss to spy,
He pass'd the flaming bounds of place and time:§
The living throne, the sapphire-blaze,‖
Where angels tremble while they gaze, 100

---

† Shakespeare. ‡ Milton.
§ ------flammantia mœnia mundi. *Lucretius.*
‖ For the spirit of the living creature was in the wheels. And above the firmament, that was over their heads, was the likeness of a throne, as the appearance of a sapphire stone.------
This was the appearance of the glory of the Lord.
Ezekiel i. 20, 26, 28.

He saw, but, blasted with excess of light,
Clos'd his eyes in endless night.*
Behold where Dryden's less presumptuous car
Wide o'er the fields of glory bear
Two coursers of ethereal race,†
With necks in thunder cloath'd ‡ and long-resounding [pace.

III. 3.

Hark! his hands the lyre explore!
Bright-ey'd Fancy, hov'ring o'er,
Scatters from her pictur'd urn
Thoughts that breathe and words that burn;§
But ah! 'tis heard no more‖—
Oh, lyre divine! what dying spirit
Wakes thee now? tho' he inherit
Nor the pride nor ample pinion
That the Theban eagle bear,¶
Sailing with supreme dominion
Thro' the azure deep of air,
Yet oft' before his infant eyes would run
Such forms as glitter in the Muse's ray
With orient hues, unborrow'd of the sun;
Yet shall he mount, and keep his distant way
Beyond the limits of a vulgar fate,
Beneath the good how far—but far above the great.

---

* Ὀφθαλμῶν μὲν ἄμερσε· δίδου δ' ἡδεῖαν ἀοιδήν.
       Homer's Odyssey.
† Meant to express the stately march and sounding energy of Dryden's rhymes.
‡ Hast thou cloathed his neck with thunder? *Job.*
§ Words that weep and tears that speak. *Cowley.*
‖ We have had in our language no other odes of the sublime kind than that of Dryden on St. Cecilia's day; for Cowley, who had his merit, yet wanted judgment, style, and harmony, for such a task. That of Pope is not worthy of so great a man. Mr. Mason, indeed, of late days, has touched the true chords, and, with a masterly hand, in some of his chorusses------above all, in the last of Characlacus;
  Hark! heard ye not yon' footstep dread? &c.
¶ Διὸς πρὸς ὄρνιχα θεῖον. *Olymp.* ii.
Pindar compares himself to that bird, and his enemies to ravens that croak and clamour in vain below, while it pursues its flight regardless of their noise.

ODE VI.

THE BARD. PINDARICK.

Advertisement.

THE following Ode is founded on a Tradition current in Wales, that Edward I. when he completed the Conquest of that Country, ordered all the Bards that fell into his Hands to be put to Death.

I. 1.

'RUIN seize thee, ruthless King!
' Confusion on thy banners wait;
' Tho' fann'd by Conquest's crimson wing,
' They mock the air with idle state.*
' Helm nor hauberk's † twisted mail,   5
' Nor e'en thy virtues, tyrant! shall avail
' To save thy secret soul from nightly fears;
' From Cambria's curse, from Cambria's tears!'
Such were the sounds that o'er the crested pride‡
Of the first Edward scatter'd wild dismay,   10
As down the steep of Snowdon's shaggy side§
He wound with toilsome march his long array:
Stout Glo'ster ‖ stood aghast in speechless trance:
To arms! cry'd Mortimer,¶ and couch'd his quiv'-
    ring lance.

---

* Mocking the air with colours idly spread.
                                         Shakesp. King John.
† The hauberk was a texture of steel ringlets or rings interwoven, forming a coat of mail that sat close to the body, and adapted itself to every motion.
    ‡ The crested adder's pride.   *Dryden's Indian Queen.*
§ Snowdon was a name given by the Saxons to that mountainous track which the Welsh themselves call Craigian-eryri: it included all the highlands of Caernarvonshire and Merionethshire, as far east as the river Conway. R. Hygden, speaking of the Castle of Conway, built by King Edward I. says, *Ad ortum amnis Conway ad clivum montis Erery:* and Matthew of Westminster, *(ad an.* 1283*) Apud Aberconway ad pedes montis Snowdoniæ fecit erigi castrum forte.*
‖ Gilbert de Clare, surnamed the Red, Earl of Gloucester and Hertford, son-in-law to King Edward.
¶ Edmond de Mortimer, Lord of Wigmore. They both were Lords Marchers, whose lands lay on the borders of Wales, and probably accompanied the King in this expedition.

I. 2.

On a rock, whose haughty brow   15
Frowns o'er old Conway's foaming flood,
Rob'd in the sable garb of woe,
With haggard eyes the poet stood;
(Loose his beard, and hoary hair*
Stream'd like a meteor to the troubled air,†)   20
And with a master's hand and prophet's fire
Struck the deep sorrows of his lyre.
' Hark how each giant oak and desert cave
' Sighs to the torrent's awful voice beneath!
' O'er thee, oh King! their hundred arms they wave,
' Revenge on thee in hoarser murmurs breathe;   26
' Vocal no more, since Cambria's fatal day,
' To highborn Hoel's harp, or soft Llewellyn's lay.

I. 3.

' Cold is Cadwallo's tongue,
' That hush'd the stormy main;   30
' Brave Urien sleeps upon his craggy bed:
' Mountains! ye moan in vain
' Modrid, whose magic song
' Made huge Plinlimmon bow his cloud-topp'd head,
' On dreary Arvon's ‡ shore they lie,   35
' Smear'd with gore and ghastly pale;
' Far, far aloof th' affrighted ravens sail,
' The famish'd eagle § screams and passes by.

---

* The image was taken from a well-known picture of Raphael, representing the Supreme Being in the vision of Ezekiel. There are two of these paintings, both believed original; one at Florence, the other at Paris.

† Shone like a meteor streaming to the wind.
         Milton's Paradise Lost.

‡ The shores of Caernarvonshire, opposite to the isle of Anglesey.

§ Camden and others observe, that eagles used annually to build their aerie among the rocks of Snowdon, which from thence (as some think) were named by the Welsh, Craigian-eryri, or the Crags of the Eagles. At this day (I am told) the highest point of Snowdon is called The Eagle's Nest. That bird is certainly no stranger to this island, as the Scots, and the people of Cumberland, Westmoreland, &c. can testify: it even has built its nest in the Peak of Derbyshire. [See *Willoughby's Ornithol.* published by Ray.]

' Dear loft companions of my tuneful art,
' Dear ‖ as the light that visits these sad eyes,   40
' Dear as the ruddy drops that warm my heart,
' Ye dy'd amidst your dying country's cries———
' No more I weep. They do not sleep:
' On yonder cliffs, a grisly band,
' I see them sit; they linger yet,   45
' Avengers of their native land;
' With me in dreadful harmony they join,
' And weave * with bloody hands the tissue of thy line.'

II. 1.

" Weave the warp and weave the woof,
" The winding-sheet of Edward's race;   50
" Give ample room and verge enough
" The characters of hell to trace.
" Mark the year and mark the night
" When Severn shall re-echo with affright
" The shrieks of death thro' Berkley's roofs that ring,
" Shrieks of an agonizing king!†   56
" She-wolf of France, ‡ with unrelenting fangs
" That tear'st the bowels of thy mangled mate,
" From thee § be born who o'er thy country hangs
" The scourge of Heav'n. What terrors round him
        wait!   60
" Amazement in his van, with Flight combin'd,
" And Sorrow's faded form, and Solitude behind.

II. 2.

" Mighty victor, mighty lord,
" Low on his fun'ral couch he lies!¶
" No pitying heart, no eye, afford   65
" A tear to grace his obsequies!

‖ As dear to me as are the ruddy drops
   That visit my sad heart———   *Shakesp. Julius Cæsar.*
* See the Norwegian Ode that follows.
† Edward II. cruelly butchered in Berkley Castle.
‡ Isabel of France, Edward II's adulterous queen.
§ Triumphs of Edward III. In France.
¶ Death of that king, abandoned by his children, and even robbed in
his last moments by his courtiers and his mistress.

" Is the sable warrior * fled ?
" Thy son is gone; he rests among the dead.
" The swarm that in thy noontide beam were born,
" Gone to salute the rising morn: 70
" Fair laughs the morn,† and soft the zephyr blows,
" While proudly riding o'er the azure realm,
" In gallant trim the gilded vessel goes,
" Youth on the prow and Pleasure at the helm,
" Regardless of the sweeping whirlwind's sway, 75
" That hush'd in grim repose expects his ev'ning prey,

II. 3.

" Fill high the sparkling bowl,‡
" The rich repast prepare;
" Reft of a crown, he yet may share the feast.
" Close by the regal chair 80
" Fell Thirst and Famine scowl
" A baleful smile upon the baffled guest.
" Heard ye the din of battle bray,§
" Lance to lance and horse to horse? 84
" Long years of havock urge their destin'd course,
" And thro' the kindred squadrons mow their way!
" Ye Tow'rs of Julius!‖ London's lasting shame,
" With many a foul and midnight murder fed,
" Revere his consort's ¶ faith, his father's ** fame,
" And spare the meek usurper's †† holy head. 90

* Edward the Black Prince, dead some time before his father.
† Magnificence of Richard II's. reign. See Froissard, and other cotemporary writers.
‡ Richard II. (as we are told by Archbishop Scroop, and the confederate Lords, in their manifesto, by Thomas of Walsingham, and all the older writers) was starved to death. The story of his assassination by Sir Piers of Exon is of much later date.
§ Ruinous civil wars of York and Lancaster.
‖ Henry VI. George Duke of Clarence, Edward V. Richard Duke of York, &c. believed to be murdered secretly in the Tower of London. The oldest part of that structure is vulgarly attributed to Julius Cæsar.
¶ Margaret of Anjou, a woman of heroic spirit, who struggled hard to save her husband and her crown.
** Henry V.
†† Henry VI. very near being canonized. The line of Lancaster had no right of inheritance to the crown.

" Above, below, the Rose of snow,*
" Twin'd with her blushing foe, we spread;
" The bristled Boar † in infant gore
" Wallows beneath the thorny shade.   94
" Now, Brothers'! bending o'er th' accursed loom,
" Stamp we our vengeance deep, and ratify his doom.

III. 1.

" Edward, lo! to sudden fate
" (Weave we the woof; the thread is spun:)
" Half of thy heart ‡ we consecrate;
" (The web is wove; the work is done.")   100
' Stay, oh stay! nor thus forlorn
' Leave me unbless'd, unpity'd, here to mourn.
' In yon' bright track, that fires the western skies,
' They melt, they vanish from my eyes.
' But oh! what solemn scenes on Snowdon's height,
' Descending slow, their glitt'ring skirts unroll! 106
' Visions of glory! spare my aching sight,
' Ye unborn ages crowd not on my soul!
' No more our long-lost Arthur § we bewail:
' All hail, ye genuine Kings;‖ Britannia's issue, hail!

III. 2.

' Girt with many a baron bold   111
' Sublime their starry fronts they rear,
' And gorgeous dames and statesmen old
' In bearded majesty appear;
' In the midst a form divine,   115
' Her eye proclaims her of the Briton-line,

* The white and red Roses, devices of York and Lancaster.
† The silver Boar was the badge of Richard III. whence he was usually known in his own time by the name of The Boar.
‡ Eleanor of Castile died a few years after the conquest of Wales. The heroic proof she gave of her affection for her lord is well known. The monuments of his regret and sorrow for the loss of her are still to be seen at Northampton, Gaddington, Waltham, and other places.
§ It was the common belief of the Welsh nation, that King Arthur was still alive in Fairyland, and should return again to reign over Britain.
‖ Both Merlin and Taliessin had prophesied that the Welsh should regain their sovereignty over this Island, which seemed to be accomplished in the House of Tudor.

' Her lion-port, her awe-commanding face,*
' Attemper'd sweet to virgin-grace.
' What strings symphonious tremble in the air!
' What strains of vocal transport round her play!
' Hear from the grave, great Taliessin!† hear!   121
' They breathe a soul to animate thy clay.
' Bright Rapture calls, and, soaring as she sings,
' Waves in the eye of heav'n her many-colour'd wings.

III. 3.

' The verse adorn again
' Fierce War, and faithful Love,‡   125
' And Truth severe, by Fairy Fiction drest.
' In buskin'd measures move‖
' Pale Grief, and pleasing Pain,
' With Horror, tyrant of the throbbing breast,   130
' A voice § as of the cherub-choir
' Gales from blooming Eden bear,
' And distant warblings ¶ lessen on my ear,
' That lost in long futurity expire.
' Fond impious man! think'st thou yon' sanguine cloud,
' Rais'd by thy breath, has quench'd the orb of day?
' To-morrow he repairs the golden flood,   137
' And warms the nations with redoubled ray.
' Enough for me: with joy I see
' The diff'rent doom our Fates assign: 140
' Be thine despair and sceptred care;
' To triumph and to die are mine.'
He spoke, and headlong from the mountain's height,
Deep in the roaring tide, he plung'd to endless night.

---

* Speed, relating an audience given by Queen Elizabeth to Paul Dzialinski, ambassador of Poland, says, " And thus she, lion-like rising, " daunted the malapert orator no less with her stately port and majestical " deporture, than with the tartness of her princelie cheekes."
† Taliessin, chief of the Bards, flourished in the 6th century. His works are still preserved, and his memory held in high veneration, among his countrymen.
‡ Fierce wars and faithful loves shall moralize my song.
           Spencer's Poem to The Fairy Queen.
‖ Shakespeare.   § Milton.
¶ The succession of Poets after Milton's time.

Advertisement.

THE Author once had Thoughts (in concert with a Friend) of giving a History of English Poetry. In the Introduction to it he meant to have produced some Specimens of the Style that reigned in ancient Times among the neighbouring Nations, or those who had subdued the greater Part of this Island, and were our Progenitors: the following three Imitations made a Part of them. He afterwards dropped his Design; especially after he had heard that it was already in the Hands of a Person well qualified to do it Justice both by his Taste and his Researches into Antiquity.

ODE VII.

THE FATAL SISTERS.

FROM THE NORSE TONGUE.

To be found in the Orcades of Thermodus Torfæus, Hafniæ, 1679, Folio; and also in Bartholinus.

Vitt er oprit fyrir Valfalli, &c.

PREFACE.

IN the 11th Century, Sigurd, Earl of the Orkney Islands, went with a Fleet of Ships, and a considerable Body of Troops, into Ireland, to the Assistance of Sigtryg with the silken Beard, who was then making War on his Father-in-Law, Brian, King of Dublin. The Earl and all his Forces were cut to Pieces, and Sigtryg was in Danger of a total Defeat; but the Enemy had a greater Loss by the Death of Brian, their King, who fell in the Action. On Christmas-day (the Day of the Battle) a Native of Caithness, in Scotland, saw, at a Distance, a Number of Persons on Horseback riding full speed towards a Hill, and seeming to enter into it. Curiosity led him to follow them, till, looking through an opening in the Rocks, he saw Twelve gigantic Figures, resembling Women: they were all employed about a Loom; and as they wove they sung the following dreadful Song, which, when they had finished, they tore the Web into twelve Pieces, and each taking her Portion, gallopped Six to the North, and as many to the South.

NOW the storm begins to low'r,
  (Haste, the loom of hell prepare,)
Iron-sleet of arrowy show'r*
Hurtles † in the darken'd air.   4

Glitt'ring lances are the loom
Where the dusky warp we strain,
Weaving many a soldier's doom,
Orkney's woe and Randver's bane.   8

Note ----The Valkyriur were female divinities, servants of Odin (or Woden) in the Gothic mythology. Their name signifies *Chusers of the Slain*. They were mounted on swift horses, with drawn swords in their hands, and in the throng of battle selected such as were destined to slaughter, and conducted them to Valkalla, (the Hall of Odin, or Paradise of the Brave,) where they attended the banquet, and served the departed heroes with horns of mead and ale.

   * How quick they wheel'd, and flying, behind them shot
     Sharp sleet of arrowy show'r------   *Milt. Par. Reg.*
     The noise of battle hurtled in the air.   *Shak. Jul. Cæs.*

See the grisly texture grow,
('Tis of human entrails made,)
And the weights that play below
Each a gasping warrior's head. 12

Shafts for shuttles, dipt in gore,
Shoot the trembling cords along:
Sword, that once a monarch bore,
Keep the tissue close and strong. 16

Mista, black, terrific maid!
Sangrida and Hilda see,
Join the wayward work to aid;
'Tis the woof of victory. 20

Ere the ruddy sun be set
Pikes must shiver, jav'lins sing,
Blade with clatt'ring buckler meet,
Hauberk crash, and helmet ring. 24

(Weave the crimson web of war)
Let us go, and let us fly,
Where our friends the conflict share,
Where they triumph, where they die. 28

As the paths of Fate we tread,
Wading thro' th' ensanguin'd field,
Gondula and Geira spread
O'er the youthful king your shield. 32

We the reins to slaughter give,
Ours to kill and ours to spare:
Spite of danger he shall live;
(Weave the crimson web of war.) 36

They whom once the desert beach
Pent within its bleak domain,
Soon their ample sway shall stretch
O'er the plenty of the plain. 40

Low the dauntlefs earl is laid,
Gor'd with many a gaping wound:
Fate demands a nobler head;
Soon a king fhall bite the ground.

Long his lofs fhall Eirin * weep,
Ne'er again his likenefs fee;
Long her ftrains in forrow fteep,
Strains of immortality!

Horror covers all the heath,
Clouds of carnage blot the fun:
Sifters! weave the web of death:
Sifters! ceafe; the work is done.

Hail the tafk and hail the hands!
Songs of joy and triumph fing;
Joy to the victorious bands,
Triumph to the younger king.

Mortal! thou that hear'ft the tale,
Learn the tenour of our fong;
Scotland! thro' each winding vale
Far and wide the notes prolong.

Sifters! hence with fpurs of fpeed;
Each her thund'ring falchion wield;
Each beftride her fable fteed:
Hurry, hurry, to the field.

* Ireland.

ODE VIII.

THE DESCENT OF ODIN.

FROM THE NORSE TONGUE.

To be found in Bartholinus, de causis contemnendæ mortis; Hafniæ, 1689, Quarto.

Upreis Odinn allda gauir, &c.

UPROSE the king of Men with speed,
 And saddled straight his cole-black steed;
Down the yawning steep he rode
That leads to Hela's ‖ drear abode.
Him the Dog of Darkness spy'd;   5
His shaggy throat he open'd wide,
While from his jaws, with carnage fill'd,
Foam and human gore distill'd:
Hoarse he bays with hideous din,
Eyes that glow and fangs that grin,   10
And long pursues with fruitless yell
The father of the pow'rful spell.
Onward still his way he takes,
(The groaning earth beneath him shakes,)
Till full before his fearless eyes   15
The portals nine of hell arise.
 Right against the eastern gate,
By the moss-grown pile he sate,
Where long of yore to sleep was laid
The dust of the prophetic maid.   20
Facing to the northen clime,
Thrice he trac'd the Runic rhyme,
Thrice pronounc'd, in accents dread,
The thrilling verse that wakes the dead,
Till from out the hollow ground   25
Slowly breath'd a sullen sound.
 PROPH. What call unknown, what charms presume
To break the quiet of the tomb?

‖ Niflheimr, the hell of the Gothic nations, consisted of nine worlds, to which were devoted all such as died of sickness, old age, or by any other means than in battle: over it presided Hela, the goddess of Death.

Who thus afflicts my troubled sprite,
And drags me from the realms of Night? 30
Long on these mould'ring bones have beat
The winter's snow, the summer's heat,
The drenching dews and driving rain!
Let me, let me sleep again.
Who is he, with voice unblest, 35
That calls me from the bed of rest?

ODIN. A traveller, to thee unknown,
Is he that calls, a warrior's son.
Thou the deeds of light shalt know;
Tell me what is done below, 40
For whom yon' glitt'ring board is spread,
Drest for whom yon' golden bed?

PROPH. Mantling in the goblet see
The pure bev'rage of the bee,
O'er it hangs the shield of gold; 45
'Tis the drink of Balder bold:
Balder's head to death is giv'n;
Pain can reach the sons of Heav'n!
Unwilling I my lips unclose;
Leave me, leave me to repose. 50

ODIN. Once again my call obey:
Prophetess! arise, and say,
What dangers Odin's child await,
Who the author of his fate?

PROPH. In Hoder's hand the hero's doom; 55
His brother sends him to the tomb.
Now my weary lips I close;
Leave me, leave me to repose.

ODIN. Prophetess! my spell obey;
Once again arise, and say, 60
Who th' avenger of his guilt,
By whom shall Hoder's blood be spilt?

PROPH. In the caverns of the west,
By Odin's fierce embrace comprest,
A wond'rous boy shall Rinda bear, 65
Who ne'er shall comb his raven-hair,
Nor wash his visage in the stream,
Nor see the sun's departing beam,

Till he on Hoder's corſe ſhall ſmile
Flaming on the fun'ral pile.
Now my weary lips I cloſe;
Leave me, leave me to repoſe.

   ODIN. Yet a while my call obey:
Propheteſs! awake, and ſay,
What virgins theſe, in ſpeechleſs woe,
That bend to earth their ſolemn brow,
That their flaxen treſſes tear,
And ſnowy veils that float in air?
Tell me whence their ſorrows roſe,
Then I leave thee to repoſe.

   PROPH. Ha! no traveller art thou;
King of Men, I know thee now;
Mightieſt of a mighty line——

   ODIN. No boding maid of ſkill divine
Art thou, no propheteſs of good,
But mother of the giant-brood!

   PROPH. Hie the hence, and boaſt at home,
That never ſhall enquirer come
To break my iron-ſleep again
Till Lok † has burſt his tenfold chain;
Never till ſubſtantial Night
Has re-aſſum'd her ancient right,
Till, wrapp'd in flames, in ruin hurl'd,
Sinks the fabric of the world.

---

† Lok is the evil being, who continues in chains till the *twilight of the gods* approaches, when he ſhall break his bonds; the human race, the ſtars, and ſun, ſhall diſappear, the earth ſink in the ſeas, and fire conſume the ſkies: even Odin himſelf, and his kindred deities, ſhall periſh. For a farther explanation of this mythology, ſee *Introduction a l' Hiſtoire de Danemarc, par Mons. Mallat*, 1775, 4to; or rather a tranſlation of it publiſhed in 1770, and entitled *Northern Antiquities*, in which ſome miſtakes in the original are judiciouſly corrected.

ODE IX.

THE DEATH OF HOEL.

From the Welsh *of* Aneurim, *styled*
THE MONARCH OF THE BARDS.

He flourished about the Time of Taliessin, *A. D.* 570.

This Ode is extracted from the Gododin.

[See Mr. Evans's Specimens, p. 71, 73.]

HAD I but the torrent's might,
   With headlong rage, and wild affright,
Upon Deïra's squadrons hurl'd,
To rush and sweep them from the world!
Too, too secure in youthful pride,   5
By them my friend, my Hoel, dy'd,
Great Cian's son; of Madoc old,
He ask'd no heaps of hoarded gold;
Alone in Nature's wealth array'd,
He ask'd and had the lovely maid.   10
   To Cattraeth's vale, in glitt'ring row,
Twice two hundred warriours go;
Ev'ry warriour's manly neck
Chains of regal honour deck,
Wreath'd in many a golden link: 15
From the golden cup they drink
Nectar that the bees produce,
Or the grape's ecstatic juice.
Flush'd with mirth and hope they burn,
But none from Cattraeth's vale return,   20
Save Aëron brave and Conan strong,
(Bursting through the bloody throng,)
And I, the meanest of them all,
That live to weep and sing their fall.   24

ODE X.

THE TRIUMPH OF OWEN.

A FRAGMENT.

From Mr. Evans's Specimen of the Welsh Poetry,
London, 1764, Quarto.

Advertisement.

OWEN succeeded his father Griffin in the Principality of North Wales, A. D. 1120: this battle was near forty years afterwards.

OWEN's praise demands my song,
  Owen swift and Owen strong,
Fairest flow'r of Rod'rick's stem,
Gwyneth's * shield and Britain's gem.
He nor heaps his brooded stores,   5
Nor on all profusely pours ;
Lord of ev'ry regal art,
Lib'ral hand and open heart.
  Big with hosts of mighty name,
Squadrons three against him came ;   10
This the force of Eirin hiding ;
Side by side as proudly riding
On her shadow long and gay
Lochlin † plows the watry way ;
There the Norman sails afar,   15
Catch the winds and join the war ;
Black and huge along they sweep,
Burthens of the angry deep.
  Dauntless on his native sands
The Dragon son ‡ of Mona stands ;   20
In glitt'ring arms and glory drest,
High he rears his ruby crest ;
There the thund'ring strokes begin,
There the press and there the din :

---

     * North Wales.   † Denmark.
‡ The red Dragon is the device of Cadwallader, which all his descendants bore on their banners.

Talymalfra's rocky shore 25
Echoing to the battle's roar.
Check'd by the torrent-tide of blood,
Backward Meinai rolls his flood,
While, heap'd his master's feet around,
Prostrate warriours gnaw the ground. 30
Where his glowing eye-balls turn
Thousand banners round him burn;
Where he points his purple spear
Hasty, hasty rout is there;
Marking, with indignant eye, 35
Fear to stop and Shame to fly:
There Confusion, Terrour's child,
Conflict fierce and Ruin wild,
Agony, that pants for breath,
Despair and Honourable Death. 40

* * * * * * * * * * * * * *

ODE XI.
FOR MUSICK.

Performed in the Senate-house, Cambridge, July 1, 1769, at the Installation of his Grace Augustus-Henry-Fitzroy, Duke of Grafton, Chancellor of the University.

I.

" HENCE, avaunt! ('tis holy ground,)
"   Comus and his midnight crew,
" And Ignorance with looks profound,
" And dreaming Sloth of pallid hue,
" Mad Sedition's cry profane, 5
" Servitude that hugs her chain,
" Nor in these consecrated bow'rs,
" Let painted Flatt'ry hide her serpent-train in flow'rs;
" Nor Envy base, nor creeping Gain,
" Dare the Muse's walk to stain, 10
" While bright-ey'd Science watches round:
" Hence, away! 'tis holy ground."

II.

From yonder realms of empyrean day
Bursts on my ear th' indignant lay;

There sits the sainted sage, the bard divine, 15
The few whom Genius gave to shine
Thro' ev'ry unborn age and undiscover'd clime.
Rapt in celestial transport they,
Yet hither oft' a glance from high
They send of tender sympathy, 20
To bless the place where on their op'ning soul
First the genuine ardour stole.
'Twas Milton struck the deep-ton'd shell,
And, as the choral warblings round him swell,
Meek Newton's self bends from his state sublime, 25
And nods his hoary head, and listens to the rhyme.

III.

" Ye brown o'er-arching groves!
" That contemplation loves,
" Where willowy Camus lingers with delight,
" Oft' at the blush of dawn 30
" I trod your level lawn,
" Oft' woo'd the gleam of Cynthia silver-bright
" In cloisters dim, far from the haunts of Folly,
" With Freedom by my side and soft-ey'd Melancholy."

IV.

But hark! the portals sound, and pacing forth, 35
With solemn steps and slow,
High potentates, and dames of royal birth,
And mitred fathers, in long order go:
Great Edward, with the Lilies on his brow*
From haughty Gallia torn, 40
And sad Chatillon,† on her bridal morn,
That wept her bleeding love, and princely Clare,‡

---

* Edward III. who added the *Fleur de lys* of France to the arms of England. He founded Trinity-college.
† Mary de Valentia, Countess of Pembroke, daughter of Guy de Chatillon, Comte de St. Paul in France, of whom tradition says, that her husband, Audemarde de Valentia, Earl of Pembroke, was slain at a tournament on the day of his nuptials. She was the foundress of Pembroke-College or Hall, under the name of Aula Mariæ de Valentia.
‡ Elizabeth de Burg, Countess of Clare, was wife of John de Burg, son and heir of the Earl of Ulster, and daughter of Gilbert de Clare, Earl of Gloucester, by Joan of Acres, daughter of Edward I. hence the Poet gives her the epithet of princely. She founded Clare-hall.

And Anjou's Heroine,§ and the paler Rose,‖
The rival of her crown, and of her woes,
And either Henry ¶ there, 45
The murder'd saint, and the majestic lord,
That broke the bonds of Rome.
(The tears, their little triumphs o'er,
Their human passions now no more,
Save charity, that glows beyond the tomb,) 50
All that on Granta's fruitful plain
Rich streams of regal bounty pour'd,
And bad those awful fanes and turrets rise
To hail their Fitzroy's festal morning come;
And thus they speak in soft accord 55
The liquid language of the skies:

V.

" What is grandeur, what is power?
" Heavier toil, superior pain,
" What the bright reward we gain?
" The grateful mem'ry of the good. 60
" Sweet is the breath of vernal show'r,
" The bee's collected treasures sweet,
" Sweet Music's melting fall, but sweeter yet
" The still small voice of Gratitude."

VI.

Foremost, and leaning from her golden cloud, 65
The venerable Marg'ret * see!
" Welcome, my noble son!" she cries aloud,
" To this thy kindred train and me:

§ Margaret of Anjou, wife of Henry VI. foundress of Queen's College. The Poet has celebrated her conjugal fidelity in a former ode.
‖ Elizabeth Widville, wife of Henry IV. (hence called the paler Rose, as being of the house of York.) She added to the foundation of Margaret of Anjou.
¶ Henry VI. and VII. the former the founder of King's, the latter the greatest benefactor to Trinity-college.
* Countess of Richmond and Derby, the mother of Henry VII. foundress of St. John's and Christ's Colleges.

ODES. 57

"   Pleas'd in thy lineaments we trace
"   A Tudor's † fire, a Beaufort's grace.   70
"   Thy lib'ral heart, thy judging eye,
"   The flow'r unheeded shall descry,
"   And bid it round heav'n's altars shed
"   The fragrance of its blushing head;
"   Shall raise from earth the latent gem   75
"   To glitter on the diadem.

VII.

"   Lo! Granta waits to lead her blooming band;
"   Not obvious, not obtrusive, she
"   No vulgar praise no venal incense flings,
"   Nor dares with courtly tongue refin'd   80
"   Profane thy inborne royalty of mind:
"   She reveres herself and thee.
"   With modest pride to grace thy youthful brow
"   The laureate wreath * that Cecil wore she brings,
"   And to thy just thy gentle hand   85
"   Submits the fasces of her sway;
"   While spirits blest above, and men below,
"   Join with glad voice the loud symphonious lay.

VIII.

"   Thro' the wild waves, as they roar,
"   With watchful eye, and dauntless mien,   90
"   Thy steady course of honour keep,
"   Nor fear the rock nor seek the shore:
"   The star of Brunswick smiles serene,
"   And gilds the horrors of the deep."   95

† The Countess was a Beaufort, and married to a Tudor; hence the application of this line to the Duke of Grafton, who claims descent from both these families.
  * Lord Treasurer Burleigh was Chancellor of the University in the reign of Queen Elizabeth.

MISCELLANIES.

A LONG STORY.

Advertisement.

MR. GRAY'S Elegy, previous to its publication, was handed about in MS. and had, amongst other admirers, the Lady Cobham, who resided in the mansion-house at Stoke-Pogeis. The performance inducing her to wish for the Author's acquaintance, Lady Schaub and Miss Speed, then at her house, undertook to introduce her to it. These two ladies waited upon the Author at his aunt's solitary habitation, where he at that time resided, and not finding him at home, they left a card behind them. Mr. Gray, surprised at such a compliment, returned the visit; and as the beginning of this intercourse bore some appearance of romance, he gave the humorous and lively account of it which the Long Story contains.

IN Britain's isle, no matter where,
  An ancient pile of building stands;*
The Huntingdons and Hattons there
Employ'd the pow'r of Fairy hands.   4
  To raise the ceiling's fretted height,
Each pannel in atchievements clothing,
Rich windows that exclude the light,
And passages that lead to nothing.   8
  Full oft within the spacious walls,
When he had fifty winters o'er him,
My grave Lord-Keeper† led the brawls:
The seal and maces danc'd before him.   12
  His bushy beard and shoe-strings green,
His high-crown'd hat and satin doublet,
Mov'd the stout heart of England's queen,
Tho' Pope and Spaniard could not trouble it.   16

---

* The mansion-house at Stoke-Pogeis, then in the possession of Viscountess Cobham. The style of building which we now call Queen Elizabeth's, is here admirably described, both with regard to its beauties and defects; and the third and fourth stanzas delineate the fantastic manners of her time with equal truth and humour. The house formerly belonged to the Earls of Huntingdon and the family of Hatton.

† Sir Christopher Hatton, promoted by Queen Elizabeth for his graceful person and fine dancing.----Brawls were a sort of a figure-dance then in vogue, and probably deemed as elegant as our modern cotillons, or still more modern quadrilles.

What, in the very firſt beginning?
Shame of the verſifying tribe!
Your hiſt'ry whither are you ſpinning?
Can you do nothing but deſcribe?
    A houſe there is (and that's enough)
From whence one fatal morning iſſues
A brace of warriors,† not in buff,
But ruſtling in their ſilks and tiſſues.
    The firſt came *cap à-pée* from France,
Her conq'ring deſtiny fulfilling,
Whom meaner beauties eye aſkance,
And vainly ape her art of killing.
    The other Amazon kind Heav'n
Had arm'd with ſpirit, wit, and ſatire;
But Cobham had the poliſh giv'n,
And tipp'd her arrows with good-nature.
    To celebrate her eyes, her air—
Coarſe panegyrics would but teaſe her?
Meliſſa is her *nom de guerre*;
Alas! who would not wiſh to pleaſe her?
    With bonnet blue and capuchine,
And aprons long, they hid their armour,
And veil'd their weapons bright and keen
In pity to the country farmer.
    Fame, in the ſhape of Mr. P—t,‡
(By this time all the pariſh know it)
Had told that thereabouts there lurk'd
A wicked imp they call a Poet,
    Who prowl'd the country far and near,
Bewitch'd the children of the peaſants,
Dry'd up the cows and lam'd the deer,
And ſuck'd the eggs and kill the pheaſants.

† The reader is already apprized who theſe ladies were; the two deſcriptions are prettily contraſted; and nothing can be more happily turned than the compliment to Lady Cobham in the eighth ſtanza.

‡ I have been told that this gentleman, a neighbour and acquaintance of Mr. Gray's in the country, was much diſpleaſed at the liberty here taken with his name, yet ſurely without any great reaſon.

My Lady heard their joint petition,
Swore by her coronet and ermine,
She'd issue out her high commission
To rid the manor of such vermine. 52
 The heroines undertook the task;
Thro' lanes unknown, o'er styles they ventur'd,
Rapp'd at the door, nor stay'd to ask,
But bounce into the parlour enter'd. 56
 The trembling family they daunt;
They flirt, they sing, they laugh, they tattle,
Rummage his mother, pinch his aunt,
And up stairs in a whirlwind rattle. 60
 Each hole and cupboard they explore,
Each creek and cranny of his chamber,
Run hurry scurry round the floor,
And o'er the bed and tester clamber; 64
 Into the drawers and china pry,
Papers and books, a huge imbroglio!
Under a tea-cup he might lie,
Or creas'd like dog's-ears in a folio. 68
 On the first marching of the troops,
The Muses, hopeless of his pardon,
Convey'd him underneath their hoops
To a small closet in the garden. 72
 So Rumour says; (who will believe?)
But that they left the door a jar,
Where safe, and laughing in his sleeve,
He heard the distant din of war. 76
 Short was his joy: he little knew
The pow'r of magic was no fable;
Out of the window wisk they flew,
But left a spell upon the table. 80
 The words too eager to unriddle,
The Poet felt a strange disorder;
Transparent birdlime form'd the middle,
And chains invisible the border. 84
 So cunning was the apparatus,
The pow'rful pot-hooks did so move him,
That will-he, nill-he, to the great house
He went as if the devil drove him. 88

Yet on his way (no sign of grace,
For folks in fear are apt to pray)
To Phœbus he preferr'd his case,
And begg'd his aid that dreadful day.
    The godhead would have back'd his quarrel:
But with a blush, on recollection,
Own'd that his quiver and his laurel
'Gainst four such eyes were no protection.
    The court was sat, the culprit there;
Forth from their gloomy mansions creeping,
The Lady Janes and Joans repair,
And from the gallery stand peeping:
    Such as in silence of the night
Come (sweep) along some winding entry,
(Styack† has often seen the sight)
Or at the chapel-door stand sentry;
    In peaked hoods and mantles tarnish'd,
Sour visages enough to scare ye,
High dames of honour once that garnish'd
The drawing-room of fierce Queen Mary!
    The peeress comes: the audience stare,
And doff their hats with due submission;
She curt'sies, as she takes her chair,
To all the people of condition.
    The Bard with many an artful fib
Had in imagination fenc'd him,
Disprov'd the arguments of Squib,‡
And all that Grooms § could urge against him.
    But soon his rhetoric forsook him,
When he the solemn hall had seen;
A sudden fit of ague shook him;
He stood as mute as poor Macleane.‖
    Yet something he was heard to mutter,
"How in the park, beneath an old-tree,
"(Without design to hurt the butter,
"Or any malice to the poultry,)

† The Housekeeper.   ‡ The Steward.
§ Groom of the chamber.
‖ A famous highwayman, hanged the week before.

"He once or twice had penn'd a sonnet,
"Yet hop'd that he might save his bacon;
"Numbers would give their oaths upon it,
"He ne'er was for a conj'rer taken." 128
The ghostly prudes, with hagged * face;
Already had condemn'd the sinner:
My Lady rose, and with a grace——
She smil'd, and bid him come to dinner. † 132
"Jesu-Maria! Madam Bridget,
"Why, what can the Viscountess mean!"
Cry'd the square hoods, in woeful fidget;
"The times are alter'd quite and clean! 136
"Decorum's turn'd to mere civility!
"Her air and all her manners shew it:
"Commend me to her affability!
"Speak to a Commoner and Poet!" 140
[*Here 500 stanzas are lost.*]
And so God save our noble king,
And guard us from long-winded lubbers,
That to eternity would sing,
And keep my lady from her rubbers. 144

ELEGY.

WRITTEN IN A
COUNTRY CHURCH-YARD.

THE curfew tolls‡ the knell of parting day,
  The lowing herd wind slowly o'er the lea,
The ploughman homeward plods his weary way,
  And leaves the world to darkness and to me. 4
Now fades the glimm'ring landscape on the sight,
  And all the air a solemn stillness holds,
Save where the beetle wheels his droning flight,
  And drowsy tinklings lull the distant folds; 8

---

* Hagged, *i. e.* the face of a witch or hag. The epithet *hagard* has been sometimes mistaken as conveying the same idea, but it means a very different thing, viz. wild and farouche, and is taken from an unreclaimed hawk called an hagard.

† Here the story finishes; the exclamation of the ghosts, which follows, is characteristic of the Spanish manners of the age when they are supposed to have lived; and the 550 stanzas said to be lost, may be imagined to contain the remainder of their long winded expostu'ation.

‡ ——squilla di lontano
  Che paia'l giorno pianger, che si muore. *Dante, Purgat.* l. 8.

Save that from yonder ivy-mantled tow'r
The moping owl does to the moon complain
Of such as, wand'ring near her secret bow'r,
Moleſt her ancient ſolitary reign.   12
 Beneath thoſe rugged elms, that yew tree's ſhade,
Where heaves the turf in many a mould'ring heap,
Each in his narrow cell for ever laid,
The rude forefathers of the hamlet ſleep.   16
 The breezy call of incenſe-breathing Morn,
The ſwallow twitt'ring from the ſtraw-built ſhed,
The cock's ſhrill clarion, or the echoing horn,
No more ſhall rouſe them from their lowly bed.   20
 For them no more the blazing hearth ſhall burn,
Or buſy houſewife ply her ev'ning care;
No children run to liſp their ſire's return,
Or climb his knees the envy'd kiſs to ſhare.   24
 Oft' did the harveſt to their ſickle yield,
Their furrow oft' the ſtubborn glebe has broke;
How jocund did they drive their team afield!
How bow'd the woods beneath their ſturdy ſtroke!   28
 Let not Ambition mock their uſeful toil,
Their homely joys, and deſtiny obſcure;
Nor Grandeur hear with a diſdainful ſmile
The ſhort and ſimple annals of the poor.   32
 The boaſt of heraldry, the pomp of pow'r,
And all that beauty, all that wealth, e'er gave,
Await alike th' inevitable hour:
The paths of glory lead but to the grave.   36
 Nor you, ye Proud! impute to theſe the fault,
If Mem'ry o'er their tomb no trophies raiſe,
Where, thro' the long-drawn aiſle and fretted vault,
The pealing anthem ſwells the note of praiſe.   40
 Can ſtoried urn or animated buſt
Back to its manſion call the fleeting breath?
Can Honour's voice provoke the ſilent duſt,
Or Flatt'ry ſooth the dull cold ear of death?   44
 Perhaps in this neglected ſpot is laid
Some heart once pregnant with celeſtial fire;
Hands that the rod of empire might have ſway'd,
Or wak'd to ecſtacy the living lyre.   48

But knowledge to their eyes her ample page,
Rich with the spoils of Time, did ne'er unroll;
Chill Penury reprefs'd their noble rage,
And froze the genial current of the foul.   52
  Full many a gem of pureft ray ferene
The dark unfathom'd caves of ocean bear;
Full many a flow'r is born to blufh unfeen,
And wafte its fweetnefs on the defert air.   56
  Some village-Hampden, that with dauntlefs breaft
The little tyrant of his fields withftood,
Some mute inglorious Milton, here may reft,
Some Cromwell, guiltlefs of his country's blood.   60
  Th' applaufe of lift'ning fenates to command,
The threats of pain and ruin to defpife,
To fcatter plenty o'er a fmiling land,
And read their hift'ry in a nation's eyes,   64
  Their lot forbad; nor circumfcrib'd alone
Their growing virtues, but their crimes confin'd;
Forbad to wade thro' flaughter to a throne,
And fhut the gates of mercy on mankind;   68
  The ftruggling pangs of confcious Truth to hide,
To quench the blufhes of ingenuous Shame,
Or heap the fhrine of Luxury and Pride
With incenfe kindled at the Mufe's flame.   72
  Far from the madding crowd's ignoble ftrife,*
Their fober wifhes never learn'd to ftray;
Along the cool fequefter'd vale of life
They kept the noifelefs tenor of their way.   76
  Yet e'en thefe bones, from infult to protect,
Some frail memorial ftill erected nigh,
With uncouth rhymes and fhapelefs fculpture deck'd,
Implores the pafling tribute of a figh.   80
  Their name, their years, fpelt by th' unletter'd Mufe,
The place of fame and elegy fupply,
And many a holy text around fhe ftrews,
That teach the ruftic moralift to die.   84

* This part of the Elegy differs from the firft copy. The following
ftanza was excluded with the other alterations:
    Hark! how the facred calm, that breathes around,
    Bids ev'ry fierce tumultuous paffion ceale,
    In ftill fmall accents whifp'ring from the ground,
    A grateful earneft of eternal peace.

For who to dumb Forgetfulness a prey
This pleasing anxious being e'er resign'd,
Left the warm precincts of the cheerful day,
Nor cast one longing ling'ring look behind?　　88
　On some fond breast the parting soul relies,
Some pious drops the closing eye requires;
E'en from the tomb the voice of Nature cries,
E'en in our ashes † live their wonted fires.　　92
　For thee, who, mindful of th' unhonour'd dead,
Dost in those lines their artless tale relate,
If chance, by lonely Contemplation led,
Some kindred spirit shall inquire thy fate,　　96
　Haply some hoary-headed swain may say,
" Oft' have we seen him, at the peep of dawn,
" Brushing with hasty steps the dews away,
" To meet the sun upon the upland lawn.　　100
　" There, at the foot of yonder nodding beech,
" That wreathes its old fantastic root so high,
" His listless length at noon-tide would he stretch,
" And pore upon the brook that babbles by.　　104
　" Hard by yon' wood, now smiling as in scorn,
" Mutt'ring his wayward fancies, he would rove;
" Now drooping, woeful wan! like one forlorn,
" Or craz'd with care, or cross'd in hopeless love.　108
　" One morn I miss'd him on the custom'd hill,
" Along the heath,‡ and near his fav'rite tree;
" Another came; nor yet beside the rill,
" Nor up the lawn, nor at the wood, was he:　　112
　" The next, with dirges due, in sad array,
" Slow thro' the churchway-path we saw him borne:
" Approach, and read (for thou canst read) the lay
" Grav'd on the stone beneath yon' aged thorn:" §　116

† Ch'i veggio nel pensier, dolce mio fuoco,
　Fredda una lingua, et due begli occhi chiusi
　Rimaner droppo noi pien di faville. *Petrarch. Son.* 169.

‡ Mr. Gray forgot, when he displaced, by the preceding stanza, his beautiful description of the evening haunt, the reference to it which he had here left:
　　Him have we seen the greenwood side along,
　　While o'er the heath we hy'd, our labour done,
　　Oft' as the woodlark pip'd her farewell song,
　　With wistful eyes pursue the setting sun.

§ In the early editions the following lines were added, but the parenthesis was thought too long:　　　　　　　　　　　　　　　　There

THE EPITAPH.

HERE rests his head upon the lap of Earth,
   A youth to Fortune and to Fame unknown;
Fair Science frown'd not on his humble birth,
And Melancholy mark'd him for her own.   120
   Large was his bounty, and his soul sincere;
Heav'n did recompense as largely send:
He gave to mis'ry all he had, a tear;   123
He gain'd from Heav'n ('twas all he wish'd) a friend.
   No further seek his merits to disclose,
Or draw his frailties from their dread abode,
(There they alike in trembling hope repose†)
The bosom of his Father and his God.   128

EPITAPH
ON MRS. MARY CLARKE.‖

LO! where this silent marble weeps,
   A friend, a wife, a mother, sleeps;
A heart, within whose sacred cell
The peaceful Virtues lov'd to dwell:
Affection warm, and faith sincere,   5
And soft humanity were there.
In agony, in death, resign'd,
She felt the wound she left behind.
Her infant image here below
Sits smiling on a father's woe,   10
Whom what awaits while yet he strays
Along the lonely vale of days?
A pang, to secret sorrow dear,
A sigh, an unavailing tear,
Till time shall ev'ry grief remove
With life, with mem'ry, and with love.   16

    There scatter'd oft', the earliest of the year,
    By hands unseen, are show'rs of vi'lets found;
    The redbreast loves to build and warble there,
    And little footsteps lightly print the ground.
† ------Pavento speme.   *Petrarch, Son.* 114.
‖ This lady, the wife of Dr. Clarke, physician at Epsom, died April 27th, 1757, and is buried in the church of Beckenham, Kent.

STANZAS,

SUGGESTED BY A VIEW OF THE SEAT AND RUINS AT KINGSGATE, IN KENT, 1766.

OLD, and abandon'd by each venal friend,
   Here H———d took the pious resolution,
To smuggle a few years, and strive to mend
   A broken character and constitution.   4

On this congenial spot he fix'd his choice;
   Earl Goodwin trembled for his neighbouring sand:
Here sea-gulls scream, and cormorants rejoice,
   And mariners, though shipwreck'd, fear to land.   8

Here reign the blustering north and blasting east,
   No tree is heard to whisper, bird to sing;
Yet nature could not furnish out the feast,
   Art he invokes new terrors still to bring.   12

Now mouldering fanes and battlements arise,
   Turrets and arches nodding to their fall,
Unpeopled monasteries delude our eyes,
   And mimic desolation covers all.   16

"Ah!" said the sighing peer, "had B——te been true,
   Nor G———'s, nor B———d's promises been vain,
Far other scenes than this had grac'd our view,
   And realiz'd the horrors which we feign.   20

"Purg'd by the sword, and purify'd by fire,
   Then had we seen proud London's hated walls:
Owls should have hooted in St. Peter's choir,
   And foxes stunk and litter'd in St. Paul's."   24

TRANSLATION FROM STATIUS.

THIRD in the labours of the disk came on,
   With sturdy step and flow, Hippomedon;
Artful and strong he pois'd the well known weight,
By Phlegy as warn'd, and fir'd by Mnestheus' fate,
That to avoid and this to emulate.   5
His vig'rous arm he try'd before he flung,
Brac'd all his nerves and ev'ry sinew strung,

Then with a tempest's whirl and wary eye
Purfu'd his caft, and hurl'd the orb on high;
The orb on high, tenacious of its courfe,　　　10
True to the mighty arm that gave it force,
Far overleaps all bound, and joys to fee
Its ancient lord fecure of victory:
The theatre's green height and woody wall
Tremble ere it precipitates its fall;　　　15
The pond'rous mafs finks in the cleaving ground,
While vales and woods and echoing hills rebound.
As when from Ætna's fmoaking fummit broke,
The eyelefs Cyclops heav'd the craggy rock,
Where Ocean frets beneath the dafhing oar,　　　20
And parting furges round the veffel roar;
'Twas there he aim'd the meditated harm,
And fcarce Ulyffes 'fcap'd his giant arm.
A tiger's pride the victor bore away,
With native fpots and artful labour gay,　　　25
A fhining border round the margin roll'd,
And calm'd the terrors of his claws in gold.　　　27
　　Cambridge, May 8th, 1736.

GRAY OF HIMSELF.

TOO poor for a bribe, and too proud to importune,
　　He had not the method of making a fortune;
Could love and could hate, fo was thought fomething odd;
No very great wit, he believ'd in a God:
A poft or a penfion he did not defire,
But left church and ftate to Charles Townfhend and
　　Squire.

POEMATA.

ELEGIAC VERSES

Occasioned by the Sight of the Plains where the Battle of Trebia was fought.

QUA Trebie glaucas salices intersecat undâ,
  Arvaque Romanis nobilitata malis.
Visus adhuc amnis veteri de clade rubere,
  Et suspirantes ducere mæstus aquas;
Maurorumque ala, et nigræ increbrescere turmæ,
  Et pulsa Ausonidum ripa sonare fugâ.   6

DESCRIPTION

OF THE

Sudden rising of Monte Nuovo, near Puzzoli, and of the Destruction which attended it.*

NEC procul infelix se tollit in æthera Gaurus,
  Prospiciens vitreum lugenti vertice pontum:
Tristior ille diu, et veteri desuetus olivâ
Gaurus, pampineæque eheu jam nescius umbræ;
Horrendi tam sæva premit vicinia montis,   5
Attonitumque urget latus, exuritque ferentem.
  Nam fama est olim, mediâ dum rura silebant
Nocte, Deo victa, et molli perfusa quiete,
Infremuisse æquor ponti auditamque per omnes
Latè tellurem surdùm immugire cavernas: 10
Quo sonitu nemora alta tremunt; tremit excita tuto
Parthenopæa sinu, flammantisque ora Vesevi.
At subitò se aperire solum, vastosque recessus
Tandere sub pedibus, nigrâque voragine fauces;
Dum piceas cinerum glomerare sub æthere nubes   15
Vorticibus rapidis, ardentique imbre procellam.
Præcipites fugere feræ, perque avia longè
Sylvarum fugit pastor, juga per deserta,
Ah, miser! increpitans sæpè altâ voce per umbram
Nequicquam natos, creditque audire sequentes.   20
Atque ille excelso rupis de vertice solus

* See Sandy's Travels, B. iv. p. 275---278.

Refpectans notafque domos, et dulcia regna,
Nil ufquàm videt infelix præter mare trifti
Lumine percuffum, et pallentes fulphure campos,
Fumumque, flammafque, rotataque turbine faxa. 25
 Quin ubi detonuit fragor, et lux reddita cœlo;
Mæftos confluere agricolas, paffuque videres
Tandem iterum timido deferta requirere tacta:
Sperantes, fi forte oculis fi forte darentur
Uxorum cineres, miferorum veoffa parentum 30
(Tenuia, fed tanti faltem folatia luctus)
Unà colligere et juftà componere in urnâ.
Uxorum nufquam cineres, nufquam offa parentum
(Spemmiferam!) affuetofve Lares, Tautrura videbunt.
Quippe ubi planities campi diffufa jacebat; 35
Mons novus: ille fupercilium, frontemque favillâ
Incanum oftentans, ambuftis cautibus, æquor
Subjectum, ftragemque fuam, mæfta arva, minaci
Defpicit imperio, folcque in littore regnat.
 Hinc infame loci nomen, multofque per annos 40
Immemor antiquæ laudis, nefcire labores
Vomeris, et nullo tellus revirefcere cultu.
Non avium colles, non carmine matutino
Paftorum refonare; adeò undique dirus habebat
Informes latè horror agros faltuque vacantes. 45
Sæpius et longé detorquens navita proram
Monftrabat digito littus, fævæque revolvens
Funera narrabat noctis, veteremque ruinam.
 Montis adhuc facies manet hirta atque afpera faxis:
Sed furor extinctus jamdudum, et flamma quievit, 50
Quæ nafcenti aderat; feu forté bituminis atri
Defluxere olìm rivi, atque effœta lacuna
Pabula fufficere ardori, virefque recufat;
Sive in vifceribus meditans incendia jam nunc
(Horrendùm) arcanis glomerat genti effe futuræ 55
Exitio, fparfos tacitufque recolligit ignes.
 Raro per clivos haud fecius ordine vidi
Canefcentem oleam: longum poft tempus amicti
Vite virent tumulti; patriamque revifere gaudens
Bacchus in affuetis tenerum caput exerit arvis
Vix tandem, infidoque audet fe credere cœlo. 61

A FAREWELL TO FLORENCE.

* * OH Fæsula amæna
Frigoribus juga, nec nimium spirantibus auris!
Alma quibus Tusci Pallas decus Apennini
Esse dedit, glaucâque suâ canescere sylvâ!
Non ego vos posthàc Arni de valle videbo
Porticibus circum, & candenti cinctâ coronâ 5
Villarum longè nitido consurgere dorso,
Antiquamve Ædem, et veteres præferre Cupressus
Mirabor, tectisque super pendentia tecta. 8

IMITATION
OF AN
Italian Sonnet of Signor Abbate Buondelmonte.

SPESSO Amor sotto la forma
   D'amistà ride, e s'asconde:
Poi si mischia, e si confonde
Con lo sdegno, e col rancor.
In Pietade ei si transforma; 5
   Par trastullo, e par dispetto:
Mà nel suo diverso aspetto
Sempr'egi, è l'istesso Amor.
Lusit amicitiæ interdum velatus amictu,
   Et benè compositâ veste fefellit Amor. 10
Mox iræ assumsit cultus, faciemque minantem,
   Inque odium versus, versus et in lacrymas:
Ludentem fuge, nec lacrymanti, aut crede furenti;
   Idem est dissimili semper in ore Deus. 14

CONTENTS.

	Page
Life of the Author, &c.	v.
Ode to the Memory of Mr. Gray, by J. T.	24

ODES.

Ode I. on the Spring,	27
—— II. on the Death of a Favourite Cat,	28
—— III. on a diftant Profpect of Eton College,	30
—— IV. on Adverfity,	33
—— V. the Progrefs of Poefy,	35
—— VI. the Bard,	40
—— VII. the Fatal Sifters,	46
—— VIII. the Defcent of Odin,	49
—— IX. the Death of Hoel,	52
—— X. the Triumphs of Owen,	53
—— XI. for Mufic,	54

MISCELLANIES.

A Long Story,	58
Elegy. Written in a Country Church-yard,	62
Epitaph on Mrs. Clarke,	66
Stanzas, fuggefted by a View of the Seat and Ruins at Kingfgate, in Kent, 1766,	67
Tranflation from Statius,	ib.
Gray of himfelf,	68
Elegiac Verfes occafioned by the Sight of the Plains, where the Battles of Trebiæ was fought,	69
Defcription of the fudden rifing of Monte Nuovo, near Puzzoli, and of the Deftruction which attended it,	ib.
A Farewell to Florence,	71
Imitation of an Italian Sonnet of Signor Abbate Buondelmonte,	ib.

THE END.

LIST

OF THE

WORKS ALREADY PUBLISHED

IN THE

POCKET LIBRARY,

Which may be had in Volumes, fewed or bound. For the Accommodation of thofe who fhould prefer taking the Works more progreffively, either of them may be had in feparate numbers,

Price only Sixpence each.

As any of the Works may be had detached from the reft, the Readers may confine their Choice to as few as they think proper.

SELECT POETS.

Authors.	Price.	Authors.	Price.	Authors.	Price.
Goldfmith	0 6	Sheffield	0 6	Shakfpeare	1 6
Gray	0 6	Addifon	1 0	Parnel	1 6
Armftrong	0 6	Congreve	1 0	Waller	1 6
Falconer	0 6	Tickel	1 0	Langhorne	1 6
Collins	0 6	Fenton	1 0	Shenftone	2 0
Otway	0 6	Rowe	1 0	Akenfide	2 0
Smollet	0 6	Broome	1 0	Glover	2 0
Johnfon	0 6	Mallet	1 0	Thomfon	2 6
Pomfret	0 6	Cunningham	1 0	Young	4 0
Dodfley	0 6	Lanfdowne	1 0	Pope	4 0
Lyttleton	0 6	Blackmore	1 0	Milton	4 0
Walfh	0 6	Moore	1 0	Dryden	5 6
Garth	0 6	Mickle	1 0		

SACRED CLASSICS.

Economy of Human Life	0 6	Centaur not Fabulous	1 0
Death of Abel	1 0	Blackmore's Creation	1 0
Addifon's Evidences	1 0	Pilgrim's Progrefs	2 0
Dodd on Death	1 0	Rowe's Letters	2 0
Dodd's Prifon Thoughts	1 0	Hervey's Meditations	2 6
Rowe's Exercifes	1 0		

BRITISH CLASSICS.

Goldfmith's Effays	1 0	Citizen of the World	3 0
Idler	2 6	Rambler	6 6

Which will be followed by others of equal Eftimation, viz.

Adventurer,   Tatler.
Guardian,   Connoiffeur,
Spectator,   &c. &c. &c.

SELECT

SELECT NOVELS.

Novels.	Authors.	Quantity.	Price.
Solyman and Almena	Langhorne	1 No.	0 6
Zadig	Voltaire	1 No.	0 6
Almoran and Hamet	Hawkesworth.	1 No.	0 6
Sentimental Journey	Sterne	1 No.	0 6
Nourjahad	Mrs. Sheridan	2 Nos.	0 6
Castle of Otranto	Muralto	2 Nos.	1 0
Rasselas	Johnson	2 Nos.	1 0
Theodosius and Constantia	Langhorne	2 Nos.	1 0
Belisarius	Marmontel	2 Nos.	1 0
Pompey the Little	Coventry	2 Nos.	1 0
Candid	Voltaire	2 Nos.	1 0
Peruvian Princess	Grafigny	2 Nos.	1 0
Journey to next World	Fielding	2 Nos.	1 0
Louisa Mildmay	Kelly	3 Nos.	1 6
Adventures of an Atom	Smollett	3 Nos.	1 6
Vicar of Wakefield	Goldsmith	3 Nos.	1 6
Chinese Tales	Gueulet	3 Nos.	1 6
Launcelot Greaves	Smollet	3 Nos.	1 6
Tale of a Tub	Swift	3 Nos.	1 6
Jonathan Wild	Fielding	3 Nos.	1 6
Devil on Two Sticks	Le Sage	4 Nos.	2 0
Gulliver's Travels	Swift	4 Nos.	2 0
Sisters	Dodd	4 Nos.	2 0
Henrietta	Lenox	4 Nos.	2 0
Joseph Andrews	Fielding	5 Nos.	2 6
Telemachus	Fenelon	6 Nos.	3 0
Humphrey Clinker	Smollet	6 Nos.	3 0
Female Quixote	Lenox	6 Nos.	3 0
Moral Tales	Marmontel	7 Nos.	3 6
Count Fathom	Smollet	7 Nos.	3 6
Tales of the Genii	Morell	7 Nos.	3 6
Roderic Random	Smollet	7 Nos.	3 6
Tristram Shandy	Sterne	8 Nos.	4 0
Robinson Crusoe	De Foe	8 Nos.	4 0
Amelia	Fielding	9 Nos.	4 6
Chrysal	—	10 Nos.	5 0
Gil Blas	Le Sage	11 Nos.	5 6
Peregrine Pickle	Smollet	13 Nos.	6 6
Tom Jones	Fielding	13 Nos.	6 6
Arabian Nights	Galland	15 Nos.	7 6
Don Quixote	Cervantes	16 Nos.	8 0

PLAN OF COOKE'S
Uniform, Cheap, and Elegant
POCKET LIBRARY.

The Particulars of which are as follow:

SIZE.

The Size of the Volumes that compose this POCKET LIBRARY, is *Octo-decimo*, or Eighteens, which is a small Degree larger than this Catalogue. It therefore forms a happy Medium between the Extremes of diminutive Inconvenience, and ponderous Inutility; and is thereby rendered as *commodious* for the *Pocket*, as it is *ornamental* to the *Book Case*. Each Volume, from its convenient Size, forms an *agreeable Travelling Companion*, adapted for *Amusement* at the *Fire-side*, and equally *commodious* for passing leisure Hours, when Nature and the Seasons invite us abroad.

PAPER.

The SUPERIOR EDITIONS are printed on a *purposely manufactured wove Vellum Paper*, so well manufactured, and from such excellent Materials, that it never varies, but always preserves an uniform *beautiful* Appearance of Colour and Texture, and, when printed on, has the *additional Lustre* of being *highly glazed* and *hot-pressed*. The cheap Editions are printed on better Paper than Works which are sold at double the Price.

PRINT.

The Library is accurately printed, *verbatim et literatim*, from the most correct Editions, in a Style of *Elegance* that may challenge Competition, on a new Burgeois Type, of peculiar *Clearness and Beauty*, cast on purpose for the respective Works, which is two Sizes larger than the Type of this Catalogue, and so constructed as to comprise a great Quantity of Letter-press in a small Compass; yet the Letter is the same Size as most of the Editions printed in Octavo, so that to Portability, are added Perspicuity and Ease in Reading. The *Arguments*, *Glossaries*, *Notes*, &c. are printed in Minion and Pearl, and the Pages are decorated with a Variety of *ornamental* and *appropriate Devices*, engraved on wood, by BEWICK, whose Excellence in that Art stands unrivalled. The Works therefore possess every Advantage that can recommend them to the Admirers of *beautiful* PRINTING and *decorative Elegance*.

EMBELLISHMENTS.

The Embellishments which accompany this *Pocket Library* possess an uncommon Degree of high finishing and beautiful Effect,

PLAN OF THE POCKET LIBRARY.

Effect, and are, without exception, more chafte, and elegant productions than ever accompanied any Editions of fimilar Works. They are taken from the Paintings and Drawings of Kirk, Graham, Corbould, Burney, Thurfton, and Singleton; and engraved by Heath, Neagle, Anker Smith, Warren, rmftrong, Rainsbach, &c. whofe Abilities are too well known to need any Eulogium. From the combined efforts of fuch eminent Artifts, the Proprietor flatters himfelf that *his* Editions will gain Admiffion into the Cabinets of the Curious, the Libraries of the Literati, and the moft fafhionable of the prefent age. The more effectually to accommodate perfons of this diftinction, Superior Editions are printed, of all the Works comprifed in this Pocket Library; and to meet the inclination of thofe who lefs regard fuperior decorations, cheap Editions are printed, at *half* the Price of the former. The peculiarities of each are as follow:

SUPERIOR EDITIONS.

Thefe Editions, from the diftinguifhed Magnificence of their Embellifhments, are adapted to accommodate the Polite and Fafhionable Circles, the Virtuofo in Embellifhments, and the Admirers of decorative Elegance; as they contain highly finifhed Scene Reprefentations, Vignette Frontifpieces, Portraits of the refpective Authors, and other additional Engravings; as alfo the firft Impreffions of the Plates, worked off in the Manner of Proofs. Thefe Editions are alfo printed with the utmoft Neatnefs, on fine wove Vellum Paper, of the moft delicate Colour and Texture, highly glazed and hot-preffed, and exhibit an unrivalled Specimen of the Typographic Art, fo that, from the united Efforts of the Prefs and Pencil, they appear in the richeft Drefs of Paper, Print, and Embellifhments. The Price of thefe Editions is only one Shilling each Number.

CHEAP EDITIONS.

Thefe Editions are neatly printed, on a good paper, and contain an elegant Engraving in every Number; but, from their Cheapnefs, cannot poffefs the great Advantages peculiar to the other Editions, as, Portraits of the refpective Authors, Vignette Frontifpieces to each Volume, Subject Prints, befides additional Engravings, Proof Impreffions of the Plates, and finely manufactured wove Vellum Paper.— Notwithftanding they do not poffefs thofe fuperior Advantages, they equal in Elegance the beft of any other Editions, and are infinitely cheaper than the moft common and unadorned. The Price of thefe Editions is only Sixpence each Number.

LIST

www.ingramcontent.com/pod-product-compliance
Lightning Source LLC
Chambersburg PA
CBHW031607110426
42742CB00037B/1314